National Park Service
U.S. Department of the Interior

Gateway National Recreation Area
Sandy Hook Unit
Fort Hancock, New Jersey

I0438622

Sandy Hook
Alternative Access Concept Plan and Vehicle Replacement Study

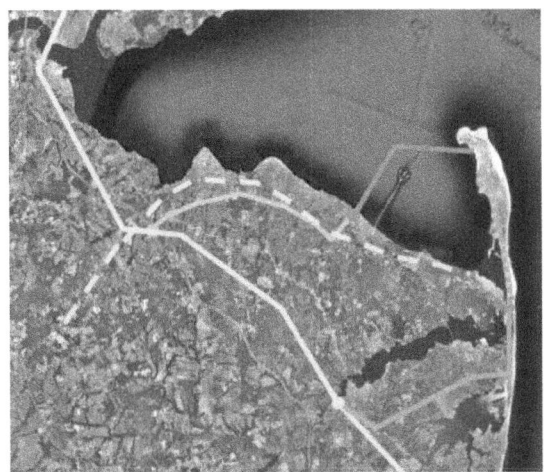

PMIS No. 133841A
June 2009

John A. Volpe National Transportation Systems Center
Research and Innovative Technology Administration
U.S. Department of Transportation

Table of Contents

Report Notes

This report was prepared by the U.S. Department of Transportation John A. Volpe National Transportation Systems Center, in Cambridge, Massachusetts. The project team was led by David Spiller and Frances Fisher of the Systems Operations and Assessment Division.

This effort was undertaken in fulfillment of the statement of work included in the August 2008 interagency agreement between the National Park Service and the Volpe Center (NPS agreement F4505087777).

Acknowledgments

The authors wish to thank the numerous organizations and individuals who graciously provided their time, knowledge and guidance in the development of this report, including:

Sandy Hook Unit
David Avrin, Acting Superintendant
Hollis Provins, Acting Assistant Superintendent
Christine Slade, Fee Collection Supervisor
William Nelligan, Former Deputy Superintendent
Lou Venuto, Chief, Interpretation & Cultural Resources
Steven Grillo, Business Management & Permit Coordinator
Brian Forseth, Chief of Maintenance
Bruce Lane, Park Ranger

Gateway National Recreation Area
Mark Christiano, GIS Specialist

NY Waterways
Augie Pagnozzi

SeaStreak
Jim Barker, Owner
Kathy Mullin, Office Manager- Highlands Ferry Terminal

New Jersey Transportation Planning Authority (NJTPA)
Jeff Vernick, Senior Planner

Borough of Highlands
Anna Little, Mayor
Bruce Hilling, Town Administrator

Borough of Sea Bright
Maria Fernandes, Mayor

Fred Brody Associates
Fred Brody

Sandy Hook Foundation, Sandy Hook Friends Group
Betsy Barrett

Monmouth County Planning Department
Nora Shepard, Supervisory Planner
Joe Barris, Planner
Bonnie Goldschlag, Planner
Anthony Gamallo, Planner

Monmouth County Engineering Department
Joe Ettore, County Engineer

Monmouth County DOT
Henry Nicholson

Monmouth County Parks Department
Spence Wickham, Planning and Design
Faith Hahn, Planning and Acquisition

Monmouth County
Teri O'Connor, Deputy Administrator

New Jersey DOT
Pankesh Patel, Design Engineer

South Amboy Redevelopment Agency
Stan Marcinczyk

Academy Bus Lines
Joe Porcelli, Maintenance Manager

Jacobs Civil, Inc.
Robert Brakman, Manager Transportation Systems

US DOT/Volpe Center
Robert Hallett, GIS Specialist
Lindsey Morse, Community Planner

Introduction

This study addresses two critical issues of concern to the Sandy Hook Unit of Gateway National Recreational Area: (1) options for alternative access to Sandy Hook during peak summer season, particularly when the park is closed to private vehicles when parking facilities are full; and (2) options for a replacement vehicle for the intra-park shuttle that carries passengers disembarking from the ferry to the beaches.

Site and Regional Context

The Gateway National Recreation Area (Gateway NRA), consisting of units at Staten Island, Sandy Hook, and Jamaica Bay, offers some of the region's most spectacular beaches; an internationally renowned wildlife refuge; salt marshes; fishing areas; hiking trails; and a multiplicity of activities, cultural resources, and educational services. The location of these resources amidst populous urban neighborhoods and sprawling suburbs adds immeasurably to their value for area residents and visitors.

The Sandy Hook unit is located in Monmouth County, New Jersey, on a peninsula, approximately 1700 acres in size, extending north from coastal New Jersey at Sea Bright into the convergence of Raritan Bay, Sandy Hook Bay, Lower New York Bay, and the Atlantic Ocean. The unit is the northern-most part of a barrier beach that stretches south and includes the town of Sea Bright and is adjacent to a region known as the Bayshore that consists of nine municipalities located along the coast of the Raritan Bay: Aberdeen, Atlantic Highlands, Hazlet, Highlands, Keansburg, Keyport, Marlboro, Matawan, and Union Beach (Middletown, Holmdel, and the Sandy Hook unit itself are also occasionally included in the region's definition).

The unit's proximity to populous urban neighborhoods and inviting beaches results in severe roadway and parking lot congestion during the summer season. On average, parking capacity is exceeded, resulting in park closings, for 10-12 weekend days each summer. These closures typically last from 2-4 hours, depending on the rate at which visitors exit the park and free up additional parking spaces. The lack of parking and traffic congestion caused by park closings are serious problems during the summer season. The primary method of assessing traffic congestion is to assign a letter grade (A through F) that describes a roadway's level of service (LOS). LOS measures the average vehicle delay at intersections, the speed of traffic flow, and mobility between lanes. The conditions at Sandy Hook have been assessed at an LOS of F[*] and have been identified as a serious congestion management issue for the region by Monmouth County's metropolitan planning organization. In addition, park staff have reported that these conditions greatly contribute to visitor frustration and have resulted in road rage incidents both within the park and in gateway communities along New Jersey State Route 36, the main corridor leading to the park.

Route 36 provides the major access route to Sandy Hook from the north, west, and from the south. The highway meanders along a portion of New Jersey's northeast shoreline between Long Branch to the south and Keyport to the north. It provides several coastal communities with access to the Garden State Parkway (GSP). At its northern and southern termini, Route 36 connects with GSP Exits 117 and 105, respectively. The Route 36 Highlands Bridge, a bascule bridge currently being replaced with a fixed-span bridge, provides a vital link across the Shrewsbury River for recreational, residential, and commercial development located on the barrier island between Monmouth Beach and Sandy Hook. On the Highlands, Route 36 is called Navesink Avenue and generally maintains an east-west alignment. On the peninsula, the Route 36 alignment changes to a north-south orientation, and is called Ocean Avenue. About two miles south of the Route 36 Highlands Bridge, Route 36 (Ocean Avenue) connects with Monmouth County Road 520 and the Sea Bright-Rumson Bridge. The entire Route 36 corridor is part of the planned evacuation route identified by the emergency management plan of the town of Sea Bright, located on the barrier island.

---

[*] Sandy Hook – Route 36 Corridor Summer Traffic Management Plan, February 2001.

Figure 1
Site and Regional Context
Source:http://co.monmouth.nj.us/documents/24%5CMC%20WebMap.pdf

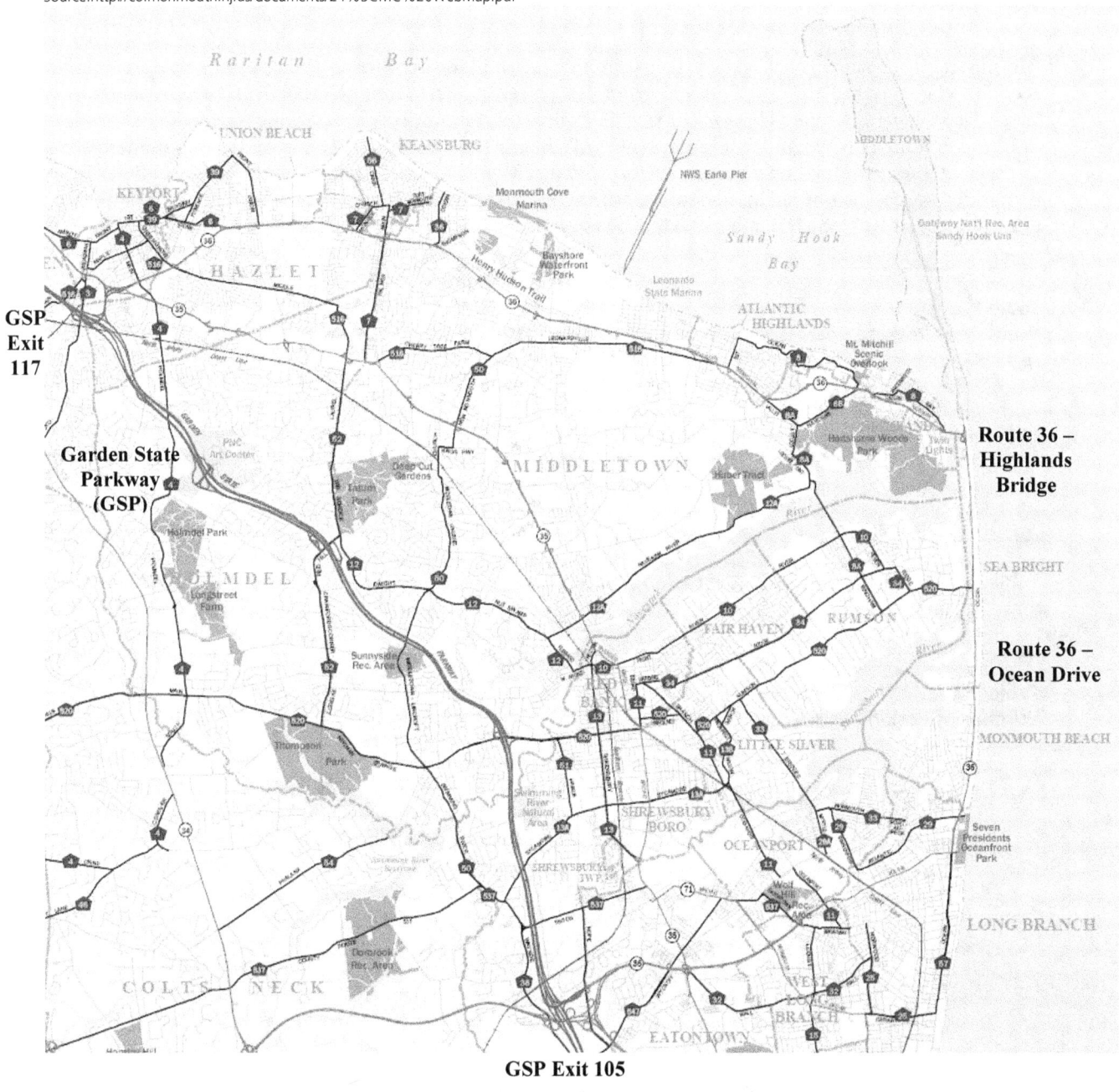

Existing Conditions

Parking

Parking supply at Sandy Hook is the primary limiting factor in the number of vehicles able to be accommodated in the Park. The *Environmental Assessment for the Adaptive Use of Fort Hancock & the Sandy Hook Proving Ground Historic District* identifies a total supply of 4,926 parking spaces. The resulting Finding of No Significant Impact (FONSI) document, a modified version of the environmental assessment, limits the total number of spaces on Sandy Hook to 5,036. This number includes an additional 110 parking spaces distributed in six new lots within the Historic District. A recount of the parking spaces in 2005 articulates a revised number at 4,819. These spaces are distributed as illustrated in Table 1 below.

Table 1
Number of Parking Spaces and General Location at Sandy Hook

General Location	Number of Parking Spaces
Beaches and Bayside	4,085
Fort Hancock	519
NPS Operations	215
Total	4,819

Table 2 illustrates the distribution of parking spaces along the beaches and bay; Figure 2 indicates where these lots are located.

Table 2
Number of Parking Spaces by Parking Lot

Parking Lot	Number of Parking Spaces
Parking Lot A (planned)	N/A
Parking Lot B	330
Parking Lot C	293
Parking Lot D	785
Visitor Center	25
Parking Lot E	769
Ranger Station	12
Parking Lot N	24
Fishing Rd. (roadside)	25
Parking Lot L	33
Parking Lot H	17
Parking Lot G (Gunnison Beach)	781
Parking Lot I	341
Parking Lot J	250
Parking Lot K	400
Total	4,085

Figure 2
Map of Parking

Source: "Planning Your Visit." Gateway National Recreation Area website.
http://www.nps.gov/gate/planyourvisit/upload/Map%20of%20Sandy%20Hook%20peninsula.2008%20unigrid.pdf

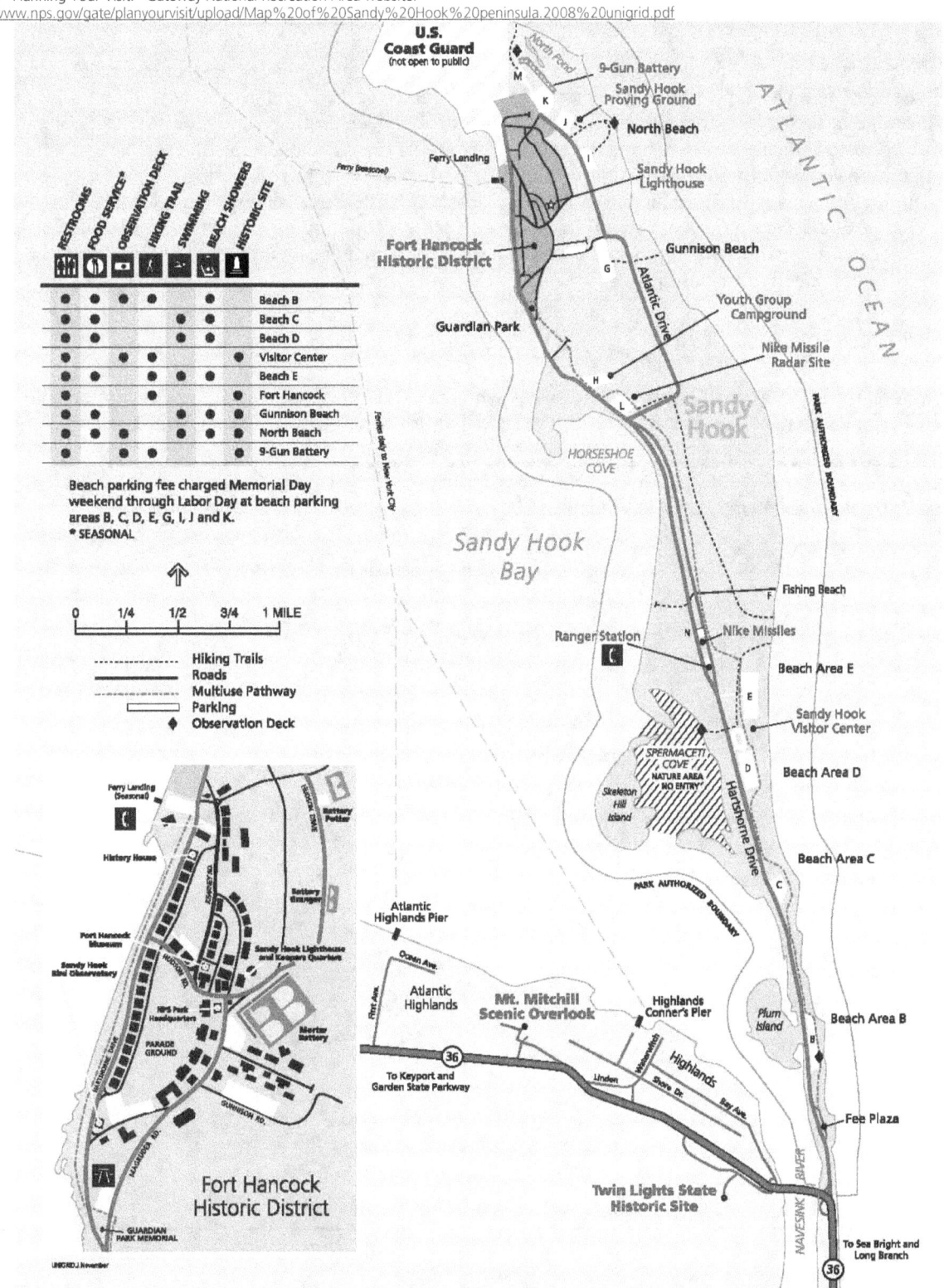

There is a general sequence during which the individual lots are filled. Although approximate, these times are: Lot G- 9:30, Lot C-10:00, Lot D – 10:30, Lot I – 11:30, Lot E -11:30, Lot B – 11:45, Lot J-11:45. When a particular lot is full, signage on the road diverts traffic to the next upstream lot.

There is the potential for closing the park each weekend day and holiday of the summer season. In recent years, the first closing happened the first weekend of June and the last closing occurred on Labor Day. On average, a closing lasts approximately 2 hours any time between 11:00 AM and 2:30 PM. A decision to close the park to vehicular traffic is based on the number of lots that are closed, the time-of-day, and the inbound versus outbound (i.e., exiting) volume of traffic. Conversely, re-opening the park is based on the number of parking spaces available and in which parking lots the available spots are located along with the volume of exiting traffic. As a general rule, between 350-400 open spots is considered adequate before the park can reopen. Lots are monitored once the park is reopened in case incoming traffic is heavy and the park would need to be closed again.

Vehicular Traffic Inbound/Outbound from the Park

Average vehicular entry flows by day-of-week when there are no closure events are illustrated below in Chart 1. Peak entry flow averages 650-675 vehicles per hour and peaks at ~ 10:00 AM on the weekends.

Chart 1
Average Entry Profile on Days with No Closures
Source: Data provided by Sandy Hook.

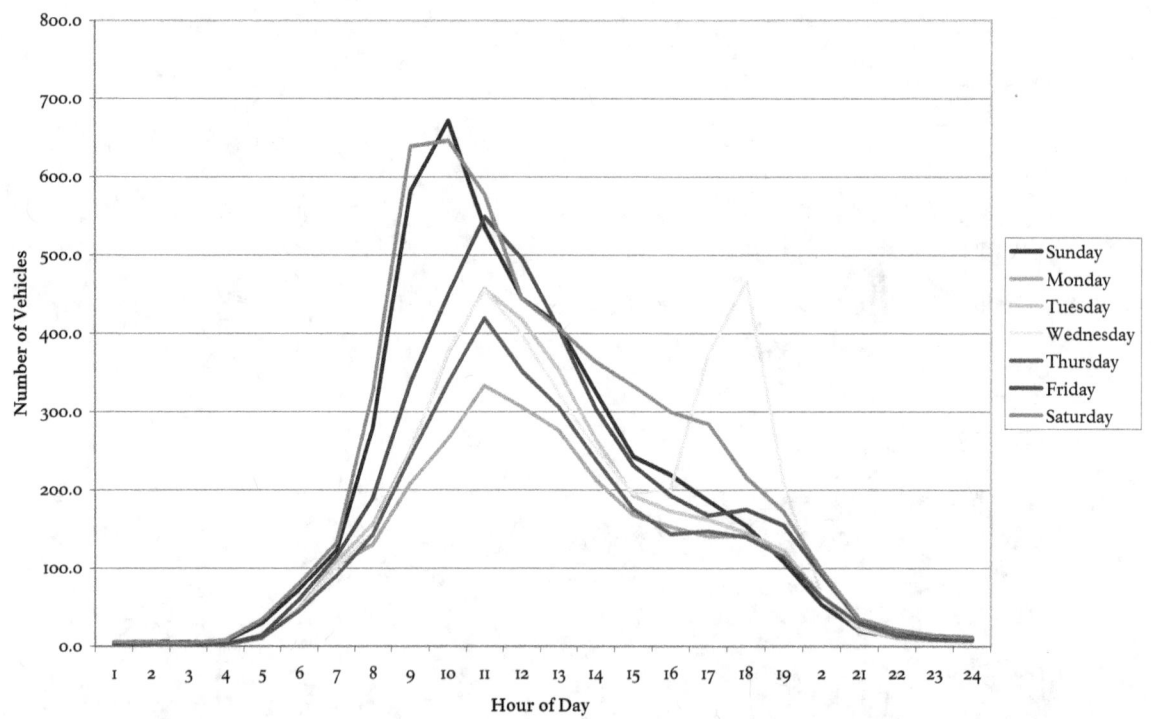

Average Entry Profile on Days with No Closures

On Saturdays when the park experiences a closure event, peak entry flow averages 1100-1200 vehicles per hour just prior to a decision to close the park. Closure duration then averages approximately 2-3 hours. This is illustrated below in Chart 2.

Chart 2
Saturday Entries on Days with Closures
Source: Data provided by Sandy Hook.

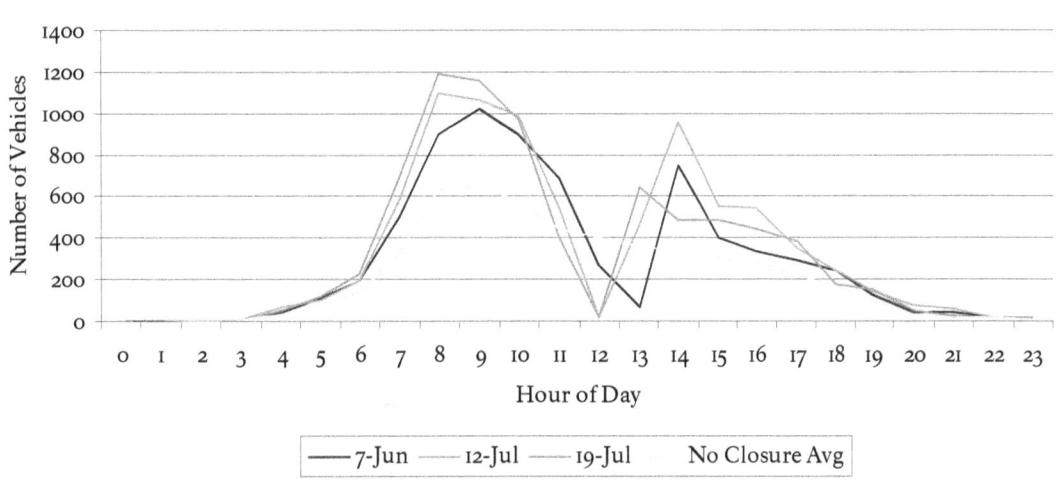

A similar graphic for Sunday closure events is illustrated in Chart 3.

Chart 3
Sunday Entries on Days with Closures
Source: Data provided by Sandy Hook.

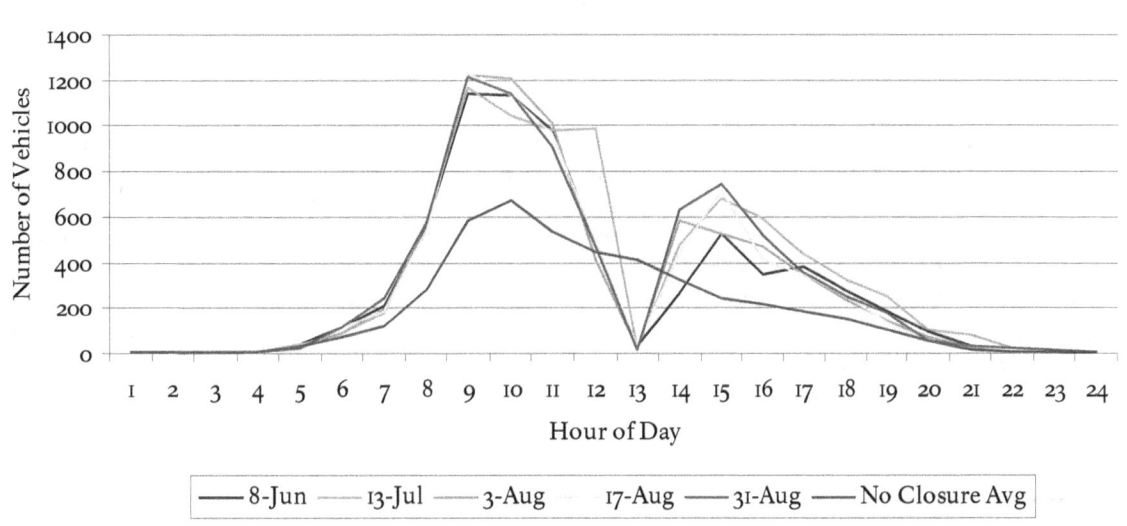

On summer weekends at Sandy Hook, vehicular flow exiting the park can jump to 800 vehicles per hour between 3:00 PM and 5:00 PM (see Chart 4). In some cases, traffic exiting the park has caused significant back-ups. Some of this may be relieved when the new bridge is completed as traffic will not be held by the need to open the bridge for boat traffic.

Chart 4
Southbound Exits by Day of Week and Month
Source: Data provided by Sandy Hook.

SB Exits by Day of Week and Month

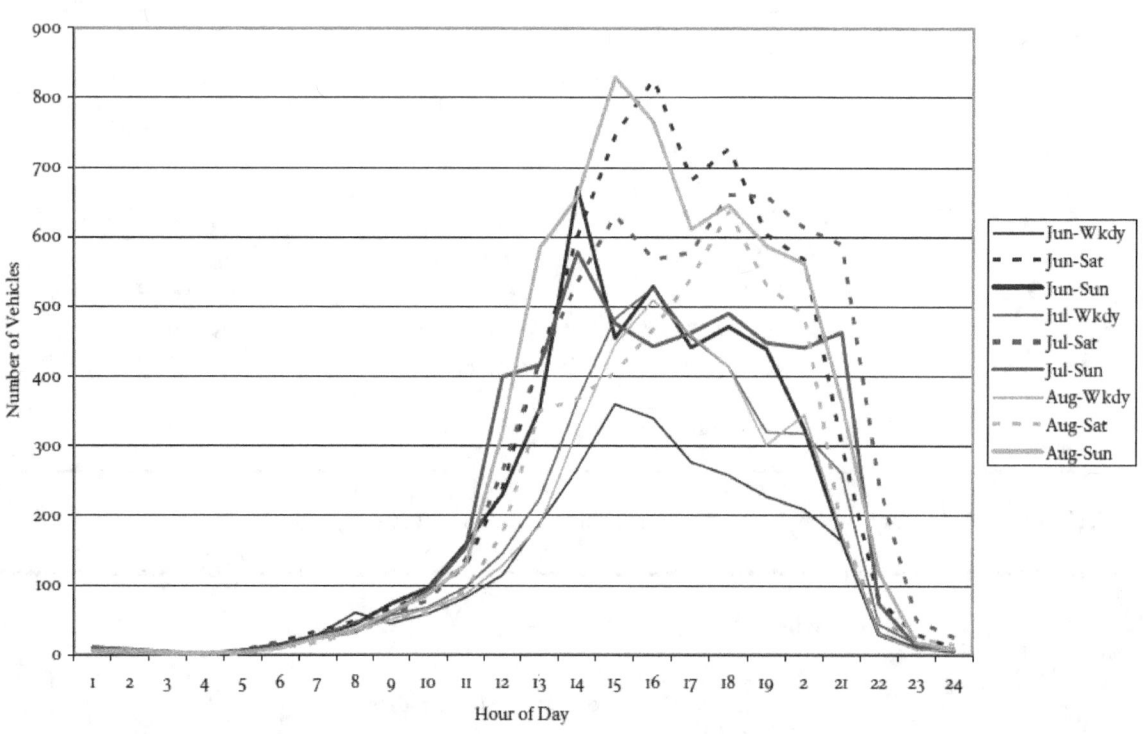

Legend:
Jun-Wkdy
Jun-Sat
Jun-Sun
Jul-Wkdy
Jul-Sat
Jul-Sun
Aug-Wkdy
Aug-Sat
Aug-Sun

Y-axis: Number of Vehicles
X-axis: Hour of Day

Route 36 Corridor Traffic Conditions

During the summer season, beach-destined traffic operates in the reverse direction to normal commuting patterns, as can be seen in Figure 3. Relevant peak-period conditions in the reverse commuting direction in the AM period (generally, from Garden State Parkway (GSP) junction with Route 36 eastbound to Sandy Hook) during weekdays (M-F) indicate traffic volumes from 1,400 vehicles per hour (vph) to 550 vph at the bridge crossing, and level-of-service (LOS) equal to D – i.e., a moderate amount of vehicular delay (greater than 35 and less than 55 seconds average delay per vehicle at the signalized intersections, and stop-go traffic conditions along the road).[*] In the PM weekday period, traffic volumes westbound in the direction of GSP near the bridge crossing approximate 500 vph and rise to 1,600 vph near the junction with GSP at Broad Street. In the evenings LOS equals C in the reverse commute direction along Route 36.[†]

[*] Je/Sverdrup & Parcel Consultants, Inc., Gateway Village Rehabilitation Project: Traffic Impact Study, 2003.
[†] Ibid.

Figure 3
Route 36 Traffic Conditions: Peak Period Vehicles per Hour (vph)

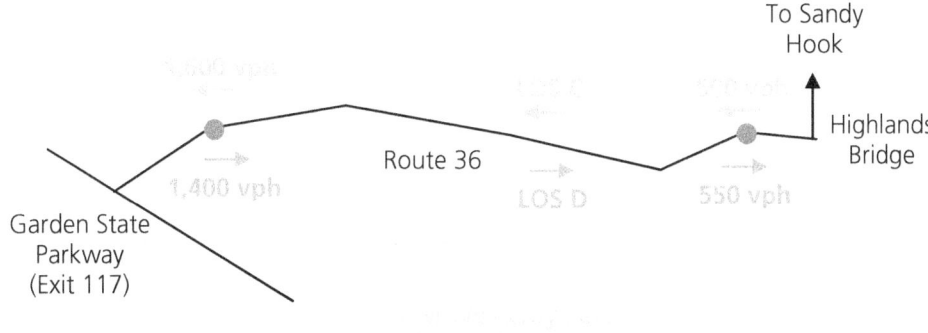

Summer weekend through-trips along Route 36 to and from Sandy Hook National Recreation Area and other shore points result in significant traffic congestion. In part, this congestion is due to traffic demand exceeding available capacity at the key bottlenecks (the series of signalized intersections along the route), to disruptions to the traffic flow from the periodic (twice per hour) opening of the Highlands Bridge over the Shrewsbury River, and to park closure events when the park is forced to stop accepting vehicular traffic when the parking capacity limit is reached. When parking lots are full, cars are turned away and become backed up along significant lengths of Route 36. Homebound traffic on weekend afternoons and evenings is also very heavy along Route 36 as travelers head toward the Garden State Parkway.

Baseline Access Options to Sandy Hook

The primary mode of access to Sandy Hook is by private vehicle. Although precise numbers are not available, staff at Sandy Hook indicate that approximately 85% of the visitors arrive via Route 36 eastbound, many who have come off of the Garden State Parkway at Exit 117. The other approximately 15% of visitors arrive via Monmouth County Road 520 and Route 36 northbound through Sea Bright and Ocean Avenue (Route 36 north).

For the last 10 years, ferry service has been operated from New York City (East 35th Street and pier 11 in Manhattan) to Sandy Hook, docking at the northern end of the peninsula in the Fort Hancock historical district. At the docks, visitors either walk to the beaches or transfer to an intra-park shuttle that provides a distributor service to/from the beaches and historic sites. Table 3 below summarizes the history of New York City-Sandy Hook ferry service.

Table 3
History of Ferry Service – Sandy Hook
Source: Provided by Sandy Hook.

SUMMARY HISTORY
SANDY HOOK FERRY SERVICE

Ferry service was first offered in the summer of 1997 and has continued as a seasonal service since that date. In early years, the service was offered generally on weekends from mid-June through Labor Day. In 2004, Sea Streak extended weekend service through the end of September. In 2006 Sea Streak expanded their season from June 1 through the end of September. In 2007 Circle Line began service in mid-June. Exceptions to this schedule are noted below. Most cancellations noted below were due to weather.

Year	Provider(s)	Riders	Scheduled Service	Notes
1997	New York Fast Ferry	1,988	60 days (12 weeks, Wednesday to Sunday)	8 days cancelled
1998	NY Waterway	5,250	26 days (13 weekends)	1 day cancelled
1999	NY Waterway/NY Fast Ferry	4,966	26 days (13 weekends, NYFF only 3 weeks)	2 days cancelled
2000	NY Waterway	3,659	24 days (12 weekends)	8 days cancelled
2001	NY Waterway	4,680	25 days (12 weekends & Labor Day)	5 days cancelled
2002	NY Waterway /Sea Streak	5,407	45 days (12 weekends; SS daily in July)	5 days cancelled
2003	NY Waterway/ Sea Streak	5,863	25 days (12 weekends & Labor Day)	3 days cancelled
2004	NY Waterway/ Sea Streak	5,291	32 days (15 weekends, July 4 and Labor Day)	10 days cancelled
2005	NY Waterway/Sea Streak	8,855	25 days (12 weekends & Labor Day)	3 days cancelled
2006	Sea Streak	6,722	37 days (18 weekends & Labor Day)	7 days cancelled
2007	Sea Streak/Circle Line	13,652	38 days (18 weekends, July 4 & Labor Day)	No cancellations
2008	Sea Streak	10,573	102 days (daily Memorial to Labor Day; Sept weekends)	8 days cancelled

New Jersey Transit (NJ Transit) has two bus routes (834 and 835) that operate in proximity to Sandy Hook but that do not enter the park. Route 834 connects the Red Bank Rail Station to Highlands via Middletown (including the Rail Station), Belford, Atlantic Highlands and Route 835 connects the Red Bank Rail Station to Sea Bright. These buses run approximately hourly on weekdays and Saturdays only.

Walking conditions along the main access points to the park are poor. For example, while it is possible to walk along Route 36/Ocean Avenue from Sea Bright into Sandy Hook, the walking facility consists of a narrow (2' or less) shoulder. Similarly poor conditions exist between the Highlands central business district, the Highlands Bridge, and Sandy Hook. The lack of safe and convenient pedestrian facilities, the distances to destinations, and the desire of most people to bring many accessories to the beach makes walking an unlikely access option for most visitors.

Experienced bicyclists accustomed to sharing a vehicular travel lane (or riding along the edge at the edge line of the shoulder) can currently access the beaches at Sandy Hook, particularly when they connect to the Sandy Hook Multi-use Pathway (MUP). The Highlands Bridge Design Review Committee has been assiduous and successful in assuring adequate pedestrian and bicycle facilities across the newly reconstructed Highlands Bridge – with a direct connection to the MUP. Monmouth County also is fortunate to have its own multi-use paved path – the Henry Hudson Trail. Originally extending from Aberdeen to Avenue D in Atlantic Highlands, the trail has been extended on the southern end to Freehold and on the northern end from Avenue D to Poporama Point. There are plans to provide on-street bicycle facilities from Poporama Point to the reconstructed Highlands Bridge, thus providing direct access to Sandy Hook. As Option 4 in the Options for Alternative Access section below indicates, the existence of the Henry Hudson Trail (with the future planned connection to Sandy Hook) provides a tremendous opportunity to increase the significance of bicycle access to Sandy Hook.

Fundamental Planning Parameters for Alternative Access Options to Sandy Hook

It is clear from the analysis of visitation patterns at Sandy Hook – informed also by extended discussions with stakeholders and park staff at the on-site visit - that the prime operating season for new transit and ferry services is from Memorial Day through Labor Day on Saturdays and Sundays (plus Memorial Day, Fourth of July and Labor Day).

There are two fundamental markets. First, visitors (primarily from Manhattan) who come to Sandy Hook without a car; secondly, visitors with a car who are susceptible to diversion to staging areas for transfer to other modal options for relief from congestion or for satellite parking as they drive along the Route 36 corridor.

Success factors for the first market (non-drivers) are:

- Ability to exploit the availability of NJ train service from NYC to the Route 36 corridor because it penetrates the heart of NYC (with large access shed) and the interior of Monmouth County on an exclusive right-of-way (ROW) absent of congestion

- Schedules that are consistent with when visitors want to arrive at Sandy Hook and when they want to depart from Sandy Hook

- Coordinated transfers between train service and either ferry or bus services so that visitors have zero wait and the connections are seamless

- Pricing that matches the ability and willingness to pay for the service

Success factors for the second market (drivers) are:

- Identification of a sizeable parking area for transfer to bus or ferry service

- Short diversion off of Route 36 corridor to staging area, and local streets that can handle additional volume of traffic

- Way-finding signage system to staging areas for alternative access

- Frequent bus or ferry service at staging area to Sandy Hook so wait and transfer times are tolerable

- Pricing consistent with entry fee at Sandy Hook and consistent with ability and willingness to pay by this market

Options for Alternative Access to Sandy Hook

Option 1: New Ferry Service to Sandy Hook from Belford Ferry Terminal

Belford Ferry Terminal

One of the major regional transportation assets is the Belford Ferry Terminal. The site consists of approximately 10 acres of land situated in the vicinity of Compton's Creek and Sandy Hook Bay in the Township of Middletown. The County of Monmouth owns and operates the ferry facility, and has made physical infrastructure improvements – including construction of a ferry terminal, waterfront bulkhead and pedestrian walkways, parking facility (~ 1000 parking spaces), and pier and docks (see Figure 4 below). Future plans call for some additional parking (~ 200 spaces), but the amount is limited by both wetland issues and local neighborhood opposition to any large-scale expansion.

Figure 4
Belford Ferry Terminal
Source: Google Earth

The County has entered into a contractual agreement with New York Waterways˙ to provide ferry service between Belford Ferry Terminal and Manhattan, with landing sites at New York City's terminal at Pier 11 in proximity to Wall Street in lower Manhattan; at NY Waterways' terminal at Battery Park City in proximity to the World Financial Center; and at NY Waterways' terminal at West 38th Street and the Hudson River in midtown Manhattan. Service is provided weekday, Monday-Friday, to service the commuter market, with at least three (3) trips during the peak periods (5:30 AM-11:00 AM; and 4:00 PM to 8:00 PM). Over time, the service has become quite successful, with parking at saturation or capacity each weekday.

˙ Official name: Port Imperial Ferry Corp (PIFC) d/b/a NY Waterways

Of critical importance to the viability of this option, the agreement between the County and NY Waterways provides that the County reserves the right, and the right to allow others the right, to use the Belford Ferry Terminal for other purposes including the provision of ferry services to other destinations.[*]

A concept for new ferry service from Belford Ferry Terminal is illustrated in Figure 5 and described below.

Figure 5
Option 1: New Ferry Service to Sandy Hook from Belford Ferry Terminal
Source: Google Maps (modified by the Volpe Center)

- Belford Ferry Terminal and ferry route
- Garden State Parkway Exit 117 and vehicular access to ferry

Access

- Market segment served: Sandy Hook visitors arriving from Northern New Jersey via private vehicle
- Private vehicular access via GSP Exit 117 to Route 36 Eastbound, exit off of Route 36 on Main Street in Belford to Terminal Road
- Shared use of already existing extensive surface parking (~ 1,000 parking spaces) during time when unoccupied for modal transfer to the ferry service

---

[*] Ferry Service and Landing Agreement By and Between: County of Monmouth and Port Imperial Ferry Corp., dated October 30, 2000, at Section 5, Granting of Landing Rights, p. 4

- Ferry terminal structure for shelter and ticket processing available
- Short diversion path off of GSP (6.25 miles, ~11 minutes) and Route 36: (~ 1 mile)

Service Structure

- Ferry distance and one-way transit time to Sandy Hook: approximately ~ 5.28 miles and 14 minutes[*]
- Operating season: Saturday, Sunday and holidays from Memorial Day through Labor Day
- Static and dynamic (VMS) message signs would be needed on the GSP and along Route 36 prior to the diversion exit to Belford Ferry Terminal. A minimum of three signs (of each type) are needed at varying distances before the decision point to divert to Belford Ferry Terminal. Guidelines for site placement and message design should comply with such guidelines for highway interchange signage.
- Once a decision is made to close Sandy Hook, the park closure event should extend to well beyond the peak exit rate from the park (~ 5:00 PM) in order to provide an inducement to visitors to use alternative ferry access as the sole means of access to Sandy Hook, and to increase the willingness-to-pay by visitors who arrive to the Route 36 corridor after the initial closure event. This would also reduce cruising behavior on the part of motorists – a major contributor to congestion within the corridor.

Benefits

- Distance and time avoided by private vehicles on the lower part of the Route 36 corridor where extensive traffic backups form: ~7 miles and ~ 42 minutes

Potential Opposition

- Possible local opposition and concerns for intensive use of Belford Ferry Terminal on the weekends
- Possible conflict with fishing vessels in channel leading to Sandy Hook Bay
- Local access on Main Street could be problematic on weekends due to limited capacity, and residential character of abutting land use. Table 4 illustrates existing traffic conditions at the intersection of Route 36 and Main St., the access road to Belford Ferry Terminal.

---

[*] Assumes 20 knot vessel speed.

Table 4
Weekend Evening Traffic Levels – at Route 36 & Main Street, Middletown, NJ
Source: JE/Sverdrup and Parcel Consultants, Inc., Gateway Village Rehabilitation Project: Traffic Impact Study, 2003.

Traffic Direction	Lane	Volume to Capacity Ratio	Delay (seconds)	Level of Service (LOS)
Northbound	Left Turn	0.91	93	F
	Thru/Right Turn	0.62	42	D
Southbound	Left Turn	0.52	58	E
	Thru/Right Turn	0.76	49	D
Eastbound	Thru	0.72	29	C
Westbound	Thru/Right Turn	0.54	25	C

Management Issues

- Three primary steps are needed to initiate new service to Sandy Hook from Belford: (1) MOU or agreement drafted between and among Monmouth County (who owns the facility), NY Waterways (the current primary operator), and possibly a secondary ferry operator who would operate the new service; (2) A 30-day public comment period (and outreach to the local community); (3) A resolution drafted and voted on by the Board of Freeholders (which meets twice a month) to legally authorizes the initiation and operation of the new ferry service to Sandy Hook from Belford Ferry Terminal.

- NY Waterways is the existing and primary operator out of Belford; a secondary operator such as SeaStreak would have to pay landing right fees at Belford to NY Waterways ($0.10 per passenger per trip). Conversely, if NY Waterways chooses to operate the new ferry service, it would have to pay landing right fees (estimated at ~ $294 per operating day[*]) to SeaStreak, which currently owns and operates the barge at Sandy Hook. Transfer of responsibility for ownership and management of docking infrastructure at Sandy Hook (post-2009) could change the cost of landing right fees. For example, a policy of zero-cost to vessel operators providing public access to Sandy Hook could be adopted.

Financials

- Estimates for operating costs were received from both SeaStreak[†] and NY Waterways[‡] but differed in level of detail and differed in value due to differences in cost structure, service plans, and the vessel deployed. The estimated operating cost per round-trip ranged from $1,000-1,500, approximately seventy (70) percent of which could be attributed to fuel cost, and estimated per-person round-trip fare (assuming full cost recovery from the fare) could range from $12.50-20[§] (variation due to load factor, passenger capacity, and other characteristics of service mentioned above).

---

[*] Personal communications, Terri O'Connor/Deputy Administrator, Monmouth County
[†] Personal communications, J. Barker, SeaStreak; vessel costs assume crew manning consistent with larger 400-passenger capacity vessel typically operated by SeaStreak for commuter ferry service from the NJ Bayshore to Manhattan .
[‡] Personal communications, Augie Pagnozzi, NY Waterways; vessel costs assume 149-passenger capacity.
[§] Percent load factor assumption varied from 20 to 75 percent and vessel passenger capacity ranged from 149 to 400.

Option 1A: New Ferry Service to Sandy Hook from South Amboy Ferry Terminal

South Amboy Ferry Terminal

Figure 6
South Amboy Ferry Terminal
Source: Google Earth

Through leveraging more than $100 million in federal, state and local funds (including substantial investments by NJ Transit in elevated platforms and ADA accessibility), South Amboy has revitalized its main street, transit station and ferry terminal. New bridge, road and parking infrastructure has been built or will be completed by summer 2009, facilitating access and egress to the ferry terminal off of the Garden State Parkway. The area proximate to the NJ Transit rail station and to the Ferry terminal has been designated by NJ DOT as a Transit Village. Substantial mixed-use development has been built or is planned for the area. The Transit Station is served by the NJ Transit Coast Line, with major origination points at Newark Penn Station and Penn Station in Manhattan. Current surface parking approximates 600-650 spaces, and there are plans to expand parking by an additional 450 parking spaces. Although South Amboy is primarily concerned with re-establishing commuter ferry service to Manhattan (~ 42 minute transit time via ferry), the docks can accommodate up to three (3) vessels concurrently, and could support new service to Sandy Hook. Furthermore, new service to Sandy Hook on weekends and holidays during summer season would not conflict with ferry service to Manhattan which would be Monday-Friday only.

A concept for new ferry service from South Amboy Ferry Terminal is illustrated in Figure 7.

Figure 7
Option 1A: New Ferry Service to Sandy Hook from South Amboy Ferry Terminal
Source: Google Earth (modified by the Volpe Center)

● South Amboy Ferry Terminal
○ South Amboy Train Station
● Exit 125, Garden State Parkway

Access

- Market segment served: Sandy Hook visitors arriving from Northern New Jersey via private vehicle or transit

- Private vehicular access via GSP Exit 125 to Chevalier Avenue to Main Street, South Amboy: approximately < 1 miles or ~ 2 minutes

- NJ Transit train and bus (local) connections to the South Amboy Ferry Terminal

- Shared use of already existing extensive surface parking (~ 600-650 parking spaces) during time when unoccupied for modal transfer to the ferry service; plans to expand parking (~ 450 spaces maximum) subject to Army Corps of Engineers and NJ DEP permit approvals and conditions

- Ferry terminal structure for shelter and ticket processing to be completed in summer 2009

Service Structure

- Ferry distance and one-way transit time to Sandy Hook: approximately ~ 14.1 miles, and 38 minutes*

- Operating season: Saturday, Sunday and Holidays from Memorial Day through Labor Day

- Static and dynamic (VMS) message signs would be needed on the GSP and along State Route 9 prior to the diversion exits to South Amboy Ferry Terminal. Signs along the Route 36 corridor may be necessary as well. A minimum of three signs (of each type) are needed at varying distances before the decision point to divert to South Amboy Ferry Terminal. Guidelines for site placement and message design should comply with such guidelines for highway interchange signage.

- Once a decision is made to close Sandy Hook, the park closure event should extend to well beyond the peak exit rate from the park (~ 5:00 PM) in order to provide an inducement to visitors to use alternative ferry access as the sole means of access to Sandy Hook, and to increase the willingness-to-pay by visitors who are driving along GSP prior to the exit to South Amboy Ferry terminal after the initial closure event. This would also reduce cruising behavior on the part of motorists – a major contributor to congestion within the Route 36 corridor – provided signs redirected visitors along the Route 36 corridor to South Amboy Ferry terminal.

Benefits

- Distance and time avoided by private vehicles on the Route 36 corridor where extensive traffic backups form: ~14 miles and ~ 65 minutes

Financials

- Estimated ferry operating cost per round-trip is ~ $2,700, seventy (70) percent of which is attributed to fuel cost.† Per person round-trip fare (assuming full cost recovery from the fare) is estimated at $34.‡

Management Issues

- South Amboy Redevelopment Authority would negotiate and draw up agreement; South Amboy Council would ratify agreement

- If an operator other than SeaStreak were to provide the service, an agreement would need to be implemented for the use of SeaStreak's docking infrastructure at Sandy Hook for the 2009 season.

---

* Assumes 20 knot vessel speed.
† Based on data provided by SeaStreak out of Belford, scaled to reflect the greater distances from South Amboy – particularly with respect to fuel costs which are distance-dependent. Assumes larger 400-passenger vessel. As a benchmark, new service between South Amboy and Manhattan (~ 42 minute transit time) operating with 150-passenger vessels is expected to be priced at $26 per person round-trip.
‡ Assumes the vessel utilization is low and averages only 20 percent load factor per round trip.

Option 2: NJ Transit Coordinated Train/Bus Shuttle Service to Sandy Hook

Red Bank Train Station

A major asset to the New Jersey Bayshore and Route 36 communities is that NJ Transit operates a very high frequency commuter rail service via the NJ Transit Circle Line, serving stops at both Middletown and Red Bank in reasonable proximity to Sandy Hook. The NJ Transit Circle Line connects both major metropolitan areas of Newark, New Jersey (Newark Penn Station) and NYC (NYC Penn Station) to this area. Train arrivals and departures at Red Bank Station are hourly on Saturdays, Sundays and Holidays[*]. The missing element – which this option proposes – is a connection to Sandy Hook and its beaches via a weekend bus shuttle, coordinated with train arrivals and departures at Red Bank train station. A new reservation system operated by NJ Transit would guarantee a seat on both the train and connecting bus shuttle. Buses would 'meet' each train arrival and departure. The fares would reflect the combined operation. Figure 8 below illustrates the location of Red Bank train station and its peripheral parking facilities. All of the parking spaces in lots 1-5, and 8 are free on Saturdays and Sundays – a total of 455 parking spaces. There are an additional 339 parking spaces in lot 9 – but currently a parking charge is set ($10/hour). With proper VMS signage on the Garden State Parkway, and with the sizeable capacity for parking at the Red Bank train station, this option could also serve the market consisting of visitors who arrive via private vehicle and who still wish to access Sandy Hook when the park is closed to private vehicles – with diversion off of the GSP at Exit 109 to Red Bank train station, then transfer to a bus shuttle for access to the beaches at Sandy Hook.

Figure 8
Parking Lots around Red Bank Train Station
Source: NJ Transit website (http://www.njtransit.com)

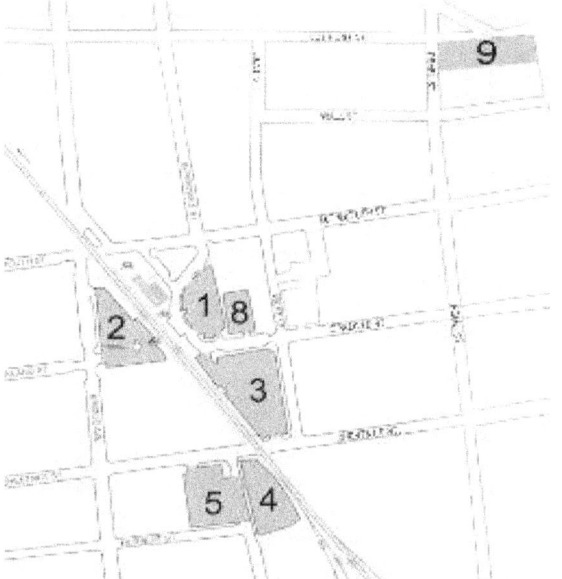

Figure 9 illustrates the proposed loading zone and circulation pattern for buses serving Red Bank Station and providing access and connectivity to Sandy Hook. The buses at Red Bank train station would collect visitors who arrive at the train station (via train or private vehicle), then distribute them to the various

---

[*] See schedules at http://www.njtransit.com

beaches at Sandy Hook. On the return trip, the buses would pick up visitors at the beaches, and then bring them back to the train station.

Figure 9
**Proposed Loading Zone and Circulation Pattern at Red Bank Train Station
(with several parking lots from Figure 8 identified)**
Source: Google Earth (modified by the Volpe Center)

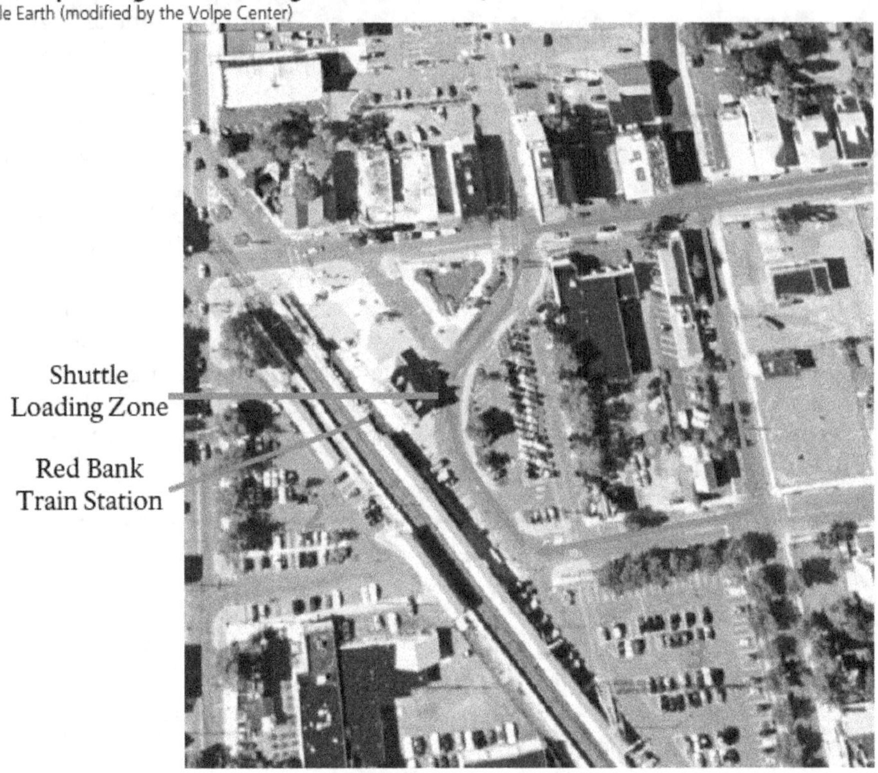

Shuttle
Loading Zone

Red Bank
Train Station

A concept for new shuttle service from the Red Bank Train Station to Sandy Hook is illustrated in Figure 10 and described below.

 ○ Red Bank Train Station and NJ Transit Long Branch Line
 ● Proposed Bus Shuttle to Sandy Hook

Access

- Market segments served: primary market NYC and Newark (visitors who do NOT bring a car to the area); secondary market comprises visitors on the GSP willing to divert to Red Bank train station for modal transfer to a bus shuttle directly to the beaches at Sandy Hook

- Arrivals and departures hourly between 6:00 AM and 1:00 AM to/from Red Bank Station and NYC Penn Station and Newark Penn Station

- Transit time from NYC Penn Station and from Newark to Red Bank train station: 1:14 and 0:56 (h:mm)

- Diversion distance on GSP between Exit 117 (for Route 36) and Exit 109 (for County Route 520 to Red Bank Station) is ~ 5 miles

- Free parking on weekends and holidays (455 parking spaces)

Service Structure

- Weekend service provided 9am-8pm, Memorial Day through Labor Day on Saturdays and Sundays (plus Memorial Day, Fourth of July and Labor Day).

- Round-trip per passenger fare from NYC Penn Station and from Newark: $20.00 and $14.50 respectively

- Transit time from NYC Penn Station and from Newark to North Beach at Sandy Hook: ~ 2:15 and 2:00 (h: mm)

- Routing for bus shuttle from Red Bank Train Station: Monmouth Street • Broad Street • Harding Road • Brand Avenue • Rumson Road • Shrewsbury River (Rumson) Bridge • Ocean Avenue

- Local street congestion can be severe on summer weekends so bus shuttle transit time approximates 1 hour to North Beach at Sandy Hook (~ 15 miles one-way). This breaks down as follows[*]: Red Bank train station to the Rumson Bridge: ~ 15 minutes; transit time to cross bridge based on ~ 1 mile queue backup is ~ 20-25 minutes; Rumson Bridge to North Beach at Sandy Hook is approximately 20-25 minutes

- Minimum requirement of two (2) buses to operate hourly service to/from Red Bank Train Station in coordination with the hourly schedule for train arrivals and departures

---

[*] Personal communications, Betsy Barrett/Friends of Sandy Hook

Option 3: Bus Shuttle from Conner's Ferry Landing to Sandy Hook

Conner's Ferry Landing

SeaStreak operates out of Conner's Ferry Landing in Highlands, NJ. While SeaStreak still operates service on weekends to Manhattan, including running several trips for baseball events on Saturdays and Sundays, there is still substantial residual parking capacity to stage new bus shuttle service to Sandy Hook. One advantage of this option is that visitors already committed to the Route 36 corridor bound for Sandy Hook can be diverted to Conner's Ferry Landing for transfer to a bus shuttle with properly sited VMS signage sited along the Route 36 corridor. When the park is closed, this option would provide the sole means of access to Sandy Hook and is likely to induce more visitors in private vehicles to divert rather than cruise along Route 36 for access to other beaches in Sea Bright or to look for a turnaround in an attempt to reenter Sandy Hook. Vehicular backups over the Shrewsbury River Highlands Bridge are a concern for bus access to Sandy Hook, but the distance between Conner's Ferry Landing and the access ramp to the Highlands Bridge via Shore Drive is relatively short. At the other end of the Highlands Bridge, law enforcement already in place would allow the bus shuttle access to the exit ramp to Sandy Hook during park closure events (similarly to how law enforcement already provides access to park vehicles). The greatest delay is the time to transit the Highlands Bridge.

Figure 11
Conner's Ferry Landing
Source: Google Earth

A concept for a bus shuttle from Conner's Ferry Landing to Sandy Hook is illustrated in Figure 12 and described below.

Figure 12
Option 3: Bus Shuttle from Conner's Ferry Landing to Sandy Hook
Source: Google Earth (modified by the Volpe Center)

● Conner's Ferry Landing and ferry route to Manhattan
● Proposed Bus Shuttle to Sandy Hook
● Garden State Parkway Exit 117 and vehicular route to Conner's Ferry Landing

Access

- Market segment: visitors arriving by private vehicle already committed to Sandy Hook within the Route 36 corridor who can divert to a bus shuttle for access to Sandy Hook beaches, primarily during park closure events

- Access distance from the Route 35/36 junction is ~ 11 miles, but 60-75 minutes during congested traffic conditions

- Diversion distance < 1 mile

- Residual parking capacity at Conner's Ferry landing available for modal transfer to the bus shuttle equal to ~500 parking spaces (free)

Service

- Bus shuttle routing: Shore-Drive • Bay Avenue • access ramp to Shrewsbury Highlands Bridge • exit ramp to Sandy Hook • Hartshorne Drive at Sandy Hook (serving all beach areas)

- Bus shuttle provides both distributor and collector service at Sandy Hook beaches from/to Conner's Ferry Landing

- Operating service span would be 8 hours – between 11:00 AM (1st dispatch from Conner's Ferry landing) – 7:00 PM (last dispatch from North Beach at Sandy Hook) on weekends and holidays only between Memorial Day and Labor Day

- Bus shuttle roundtrip distance is ~ 14 miles, and approximately 1 hour (< 30 minutes to desired beach for visitor)

- Minimum of three (3) buses required to provide 20-minute frequency of service at Conner's Ferry Landing

- Properly sited (at least three) VMS signs along Route 36 critical to success of this option

Financials

- Per person round-trip fare (assuming full cost recovery from the fare) could approximate $8[*]

---

[*] This assumes the NJ Transit cost per vehicle-hour equal to $129, and an operating service span of 8 hours and 2 hours dead-head. It also assumes that there are three (3) buses in service, and that the average load is equal to 75 percent of seated capacity (i.e., 30 passengers) over 6 of the 8 hours in the operating service span.

Option 4: Local Resident Bicycle Incentive Program and Connection of the Henry Hudson Trail to the Sandy Hook Multi-Use Pathway

Henry Hudson Trail

Another major regional asset is the Henry Hudson Trail. The Henry Hudson Trail is a paved multi-user path – walkers, hikers, and bicyclists – that lies along the old NJ Central Railroad right-of-way (ROW). The graphic below illustrates the northern portion. The ROW is a variable width of 40-80 feet, and the paved path is 10-feet wide except along boardwalks over wetlands, where the width is 6-feet. There are at least four trailhead parking areas, but parking is limited (~ 20 parking spaces per location). The northern portion currently runs between Aberdeen/Keyport and Atlantic Highlands, with the segment between Avenue D and Popamora Point having been completed in spring 2009. The northern portion generally parallels the Route 36 corridor and has the **potential** to offer scenic, congestion-free bicycle access to connect with the multi-user path (MUP) at Sandy Hook that runs the length of the Sandy Hook peninsula (~ 6 miles one-way). The Bridge Design Committee for the reconstruction of the Highlands Bridge has assiduously and successfully sought to modify the design to include wide bicycle lanes on the reconstructed bridge, with a direct connection via a flyover to the Sandy Hook MUP, thereby facilitating the proposed connection.

Figure 13
Map of Northern Portion of Henry Hudson Trail
Source: Monmouth County Park System website (http://www.monmouthcountyparks.com)

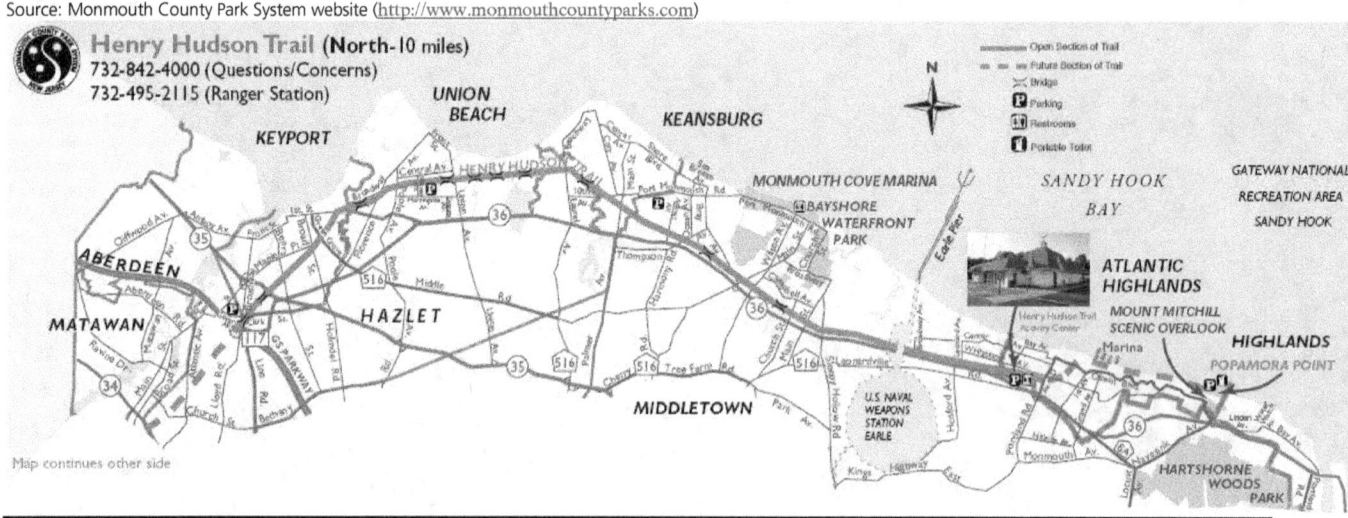

Option 4 below proposes to realize this potential by (1) accelerating plans to extend the terminus of the northern segment from Popamora Point in Atlantic Highlands to the reconstructed Highlands Bridge; and (2) develop an incentive program to use the Henry Hudson Trail for bicycle access to Sandy Hook for local residents of Monmouth County via a reverse fee or rebate program.

A concept for connecting the Henry Hudson Trail to the park's MUP is illustrated in Figure 14 and described below.

Figure 14
Option 4: Local Resident Bicycle Incentive Program and Connection of the Henry Hudson Trail to the Sandy Hook Multi-Use Pathway
Source: Monmouth County Planning Board, *Bayshore Region Strategic Plan*, 2006.

--- Henry Hudson Trail (Northern Portion)
····· Missing Connection
····· Sandy Hook Multi-Use Pathway

Proposal

- Accelerate plans and develop design drawings for both the off-road and on-road segments of the missing link between Popamora Point in Atlantic Highlands and the Shrewsbury River Highlands Bridge. (At this point, no formalized planning process with public involvement is in place). Secure funding and program the project in the Northern New Jersey Transportation Planning Authority (NJTPA) Transportation Improvement Program (TIP).

- Conduct a reutilization/revitalization land-use study of parcels adjacent to or in the proximity of the northern segment of the Henry Hudson Trail to determine whether additional vehicular parking facilities and a bicycle concession/repair facility could be sited and developed as an amenity to the trail

- Implement local resident (Monmouth County) registration and incentive program

    o Local residents would join the program by registering their bicycles and attaching a bar code sticker to the bicycle

    o Sandy Hook Ranger would scan the sticker on arrival via bicycle at entrance station and on exit from the park

- Provided the duration (calculated by the two time stamps) exceeds three (3) hours (to prevent abuse of the program), a reverse payment (e.g., $5) would be handed to the bicyclist upon exiting the park
- Program would be restricted to local residents only

Benefits

- Every three (3) visitors who arrive via bicycle reduce the demand for vehicular parking by one (1) car – leaving these parking spaces available for visitors originating from more distant locations
- Most reasonably fit bicyclists can bicycle 10-12 miles per one-way trip - ~ 60 minutes; this places much of the northern segment of the Henry Hudson Trail and penetration into Sandy Hook to North Beach or beaches closer to the entrance station within reach
- A bicycle speed ~ 10-12 mph is competitive with congested vehicular speeds within the Route 36 corridor – as well as being more enjoyable and healthy for the visitor
- Although speculative, a monetary incentive to local residents to bicycle into the park via the Henry Hudson Trail and Sandy Hook MUP could induce 100-300 persons to use this option for access to Sandy Hook on a busy summer weekend

Option 5: Redesign of the Henry Hudson Trail for Tram Operation

The northern (eastern) segment of the Henry Hudson Trail could, as part of a long-range vision and plan, conceivably also serve as an exclusive transit guide way within the congested Route 36 corridor, providing alternative access to Sandy Hook and its beaches. Unlike the other options presented, it is premature to consider all the implementation and feasibility considerations for this option, as it is intended to be a long-term plan for further consideration in the future.

This option proposes a new paved 18' tram path adjacent to the re-aligned existing trail and within the existing right-of-way (ROW) limits (which vary between 40-80'). The tram path could support an electric, rubber-tired tram consisting of a power unit with multiple trailing units. A schematic showing both plan and elevation is illustrated below. There is good national precedent (over 60 trails in the nation) in combining rail or transit line operations with a multi-use trail for walkers, runners, hikers and bicyclists within the same ROW limits or corridor.[*] Good planning and design is essential however to make this concept work well. For this option, two other factors warrant that serious consideration is given to this proposal: (1) the electric rubber-tired tram would have low impact (noise and emissions) and low speed (~ 20 mph); (2) there would be vertical separation between the multi-use trail and the tram path, buffered by landscape. Preservation of views to Sandy Hook Bay would be secured for both paths. This concept is illustrated in Figure 15 and described below.

---

[*] See, e.g., Rails-to-Trails Conservancy, *Rails with Trails: Design, Management, and Operating Characteristics of 61 Trails Along Active Rail Lines,* November 2000. Also see US Department of Transportation, *Rails-with-Trails: Lessons Learned. Literature review, Current Practices, Conclusions,* August 2002.

Figure 15
Schematic of Option 5: Redesign of the Henry Hudson Multi-Use Trail for Tram Operation
Source: U.S. DOT Volpe Center

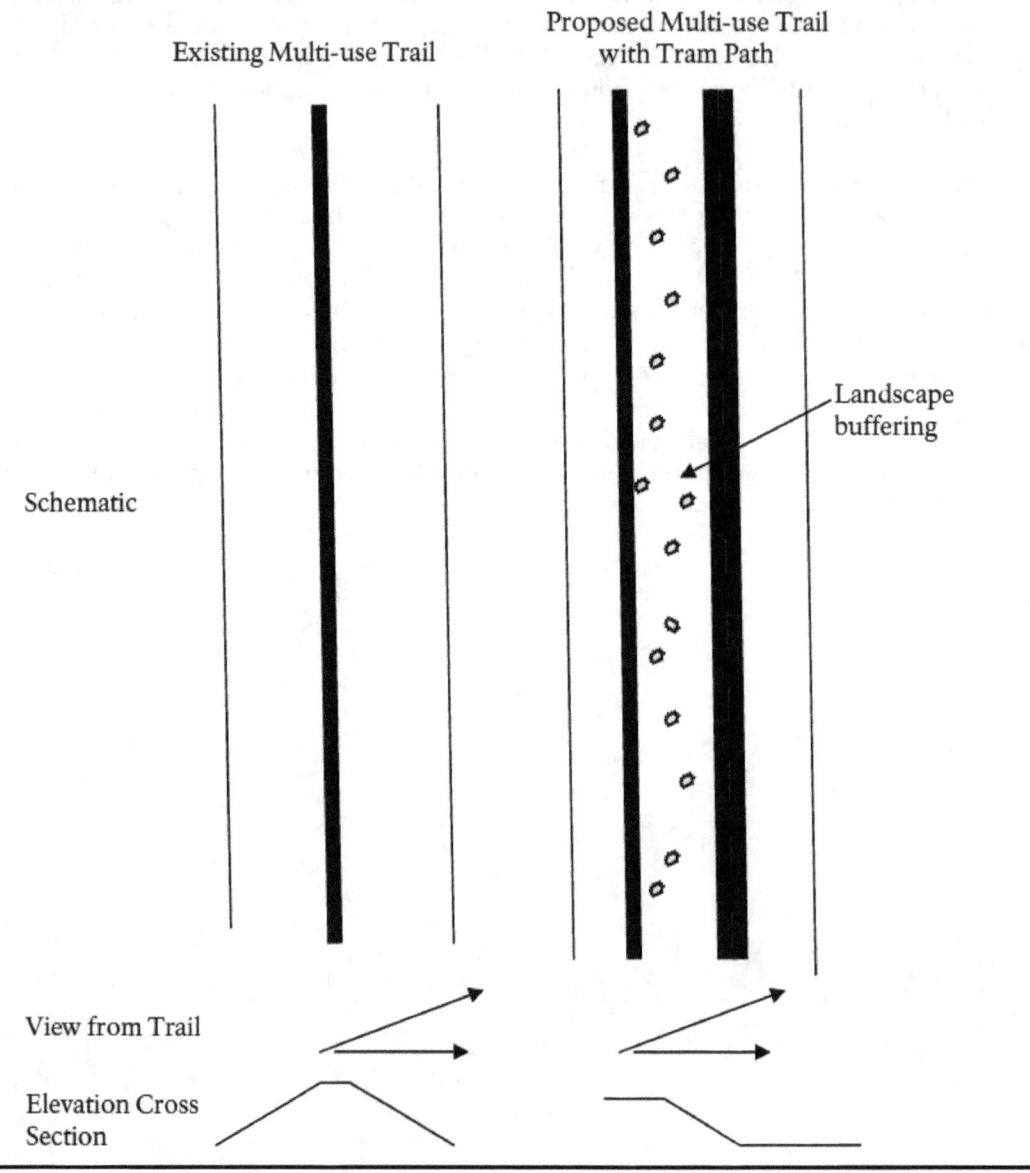

Proposal

- Staging area for modal transfer to the electric rubber-tired tram would be at Belford Ferry Terminal (with large tract of vehicular parking)

- Electric tram (see Figure 16 below) would connect via local streets to the Henry Hudson Trail

- Majority of running would be on exclusive ROW (without congestion and parallel to Route 36 corridor)

- At terminus of (new) off-road segment of the Henry Hudson Trail, electric tram would be routed via local streets and Highlands Bridge to Sandy Hook Visitors Center (not too deep into the park) where it would connect to expanded intra-park shuttle for distributor service to the various parking lots and beaches

- Transit time to the Visitor Center at Sandy Hook from Belford Ferry Terminal via the Henry Hudson Trail tram 'track' would be ~ 40 minutes (including delays at the Highland Bridge). A twenty (20) minute frequency of service would require four (4) tram units (each tram unit consisting of a power unit and trailing unit). Passenger flow capacity in one direction is equal to 176 passengers per hour (44 passenger capacity per tram unit).

Potential Opposition

- Complicated environmental and engineering issues would have to be resolved

- Monmouth County Parks and Recreation Department and local residents would be adamantly opposed unless the design solves the complicated environmental and engineering issues, is low-impact and so visually appealing (including landscaping that separates the two paved paths, and elevation differences that preserve the view shed from the original path) that users of the adjacent bicycle/walking/jogging trail are NOT disturbed or their experience deteriorated

Benefits

- During off-season (i.e., non-summer season), the two paved paths could resolve existing user conflicts by shifting bicycles to the tram 'track' and using the original path for walkers and joggers only.

Figure 16
Electric Tram
Source: ISE Corporation ThunderVolt brochure (http://www.isecorp.com).

Transportation Plan for Alternative Access to Sandy Hook

The Sandy Hook unit of the Gateway National Recreational Area is a unique natural and recreational resource within a densely populated region that draws visitors from throughout the region. Visitation during peak summer season often exceeds the capacity of regional roads and site parking facilities and congestion is an inevitable by-product. Extended discussion with NPS staff and stakeholders from the gateway communities and the generation, assessment and analysis of options for alternative access led to an overarching conclusion: there is no single solution.

A pair comparison of the two ferry options (Option 1 and Option 1A), two transit options (Option 2 and Option 3), and the two options involving the Henry Hudson Trail (Option 4 and Option 5) are presented below. Evaluative criteria are: market demand (qualitative), the visitor travel time and per person cost, and the cost of implementation (qualitative).

Table 4
Comparison of Ferry Options

Option	One-way Travel Time to Sandy Hook	Per Passenger Cost (round-trip)
Option 1: Ferry Service from Belford	~ 14 minutes (~12 minutes to Belford from GSP Exit 117)	~ $12.50
Option 1A: New Ferry service from South Amboy	~ 38 minutes (~ 2 minutes from GSP Exit 125)	~ $34.00

Table 5
Comparison of Transit Options

Option	Market Demand	One-way Travel Time to Sandy Hook (h:mm)	Per Passenger Cost (round-trip)
Option 2: NJ Transit Coordinated Train/Bus Shuttle Service to Sandy Hook	Coordinated train and bus shuttle service with reservation could induce a substantial number of visitors from NYC and from Newark (fulfilling environmental justice criteria) to access Sandy Hook without a car	NYC: ~ 2:15 Newark: ~ 2:00	NYC Train service: $20.00 Newark Train service: $14.50 Embedded Bus Shuttle: ~$8.50[*]
Option 3: Bus Shuttle from Conner's Ferry Landing to Sandy Hook	Unlikely to induce visitors who have already traveled 65-75 minutes in congested traffic conditions on Route 36 to divert, wait and transfer to a bus shuttle this far downstream on the Route 36 corridor unless there are no other options.	Access time from Route35/36 junction ~ 60-75 minutes ~ 30 minute transit time to Sandy Hook	~ $12.90[†] (~ $ 7.75[‡])

[*] Assumes 2 buses x 10 hours operating span x $ 129 per vehicle-hour (NJ Transit NTD data). This translates to $2580 per day. Assumes that load factor on bus is seventy-five (75) percent (i.e., 30 passengers) for six runs per day. It is then assumed that fare-box recovery equals sixty (60) percent. Otherwise, per passenger cost (round-trip) equals $14.33.
[†] Assumes 3 buses deployed to provide service frequency at every 20 minutes. Also assumes load factor of fifty (50) percent for five of the ten operating hours – equivalent to 300 passengers per day. Same vehicle-hour cost of $129 and an operating span of 10 hours per day.
[‡] Assumes same sixty (60) percent fare-box recovery.

Table 6
Comparison of Henry Hudson Trail options

Option	Cost of Implementation	One-way Travel Time to Sandy Hook	Per Passenger Cost (round-trip)
Option 4: Local Resident Bicycle Incentive Program and Connection of the Henry Hudson Trail to the Sandy Hook Multi-Use Pathway	Moderate cost to complete missing link of off-road and on-road segments between current terminus and Highlands Bridge	~ 60-70 minutes to North Beach at Sandy Hook from Belford on the Henry Hudson Trail	-$ 5.00 (Rebate to bicycle visitor)
Option 5: Re-design of Henry Hudson Multi-Use Trail for Tram Operation	High cost to reconstruct Henry Hudson Trail from Belford to the new terminus in Highlands to include a second tram 'track'	~ 24 minutes from Belford to the Sandy Hook Visitor's Center via the exclusive ROW on the Henry Hudson Trail using the tram 'track'	Unknown, but probably on the order of ~ $12.00

Inspection of the three tables indicates that Option 1 is more likely to be viable than Option 1A.

Similarly, a pair comparison of Option 2 and Option 3 indicates that Option 2 is likely to tap into a large market for visitors originating in NYC and in Newark who either do NOT want to drive to Sandy Hook or do NOT have access to a car to drive to the beaches at Sandy Hook. There appears little demand for Option 3 except perhaps during park closure events, and then only for several hours. Furthermore, for visitors from NYC there is a tradeoff that may be favorable to those who have a lower value of time: the Ferry from Manhattan operated by SeaStreak costs $48 per round-trip but only takes ~ 60 minutes (including the intra-park shuttle at Sandy Hook) to reach the beach; Option 2 costs on the order of $28-34 per round-trip but has a travel time approximating 2 hours and 15 minutes.

Option 4 dominates Option 5 because of the complex environmental and engineering design issues under Option 5 and the high cost of implementation. It is, however, premature to dismiss Option 5 as a long-range vision and plan for alternative access to Sandy Hook. The necessary planning and design phases within a public participation process should still be pursued. Also, a local resident incentive program via a reverse fee (i.e., rebate) system – offering an immediate and monetary reward for bicycle access to Sandy Hook – is likely to be quite effective in inducing a reasonable volume of visitors within the local communities to use the Henry Hudson Trail and access the beaches at Sandy Hook via bicycle.

Based on this relatively simple and somewhat crude evaluation, the schematic below summarizes the preferred options that comprise a multi-modal alternative access transportation plan. The plan is the composite of options 1, 2, and 4. Each of these three options should move forward.

Figure 17
Summary Schematic of Preferred Options
Source: Google Earth (modified by the Volpe Center)

- Henry Hudson Trail (Northern Portion)
- Missing Connection
- Sandy Hook Multi-Use Pathway
- Red Bank Train Station and NJ Transit Long Branch Line
- Proposed Bus Shuttle to Sandy Hook
- Belford Ferry Terminal and ferry route
- Garden State Parkway Exit 117 and vehicular access to ferry

Cost Estimate of the Transportation Plan

Option 1: New Ferry Service from Belford Ferry Terminal

Both SeaStreak and NY Waterways have proposed sketch operational plans and rough cost estimates for operating new ferry service from Belford to/from Sandy Hook. The relevant parameters and cost estimates are presented below:

Table 7
Cost Estimates for Option 1

	SeaStreak	NY Waterways
Number of round trips AM	4	2
Number of round trips PM	5	2
Size of vessel	400-passenger capacity	149-passenger high-speed catamaran
Inclusion of intra-park bus shuttle costs, landing fees, barge rental costs	Yes	No
Operating cost per day	$8,994	$2,975
Number of operating days	34	34
Operating cost per season	$305,802	$101,150

Option 2: NJ Transit Coordinated Train/Bus Shuttle Service to Sandy Hook

The relevant parameters and cost estimates (rough) are presented below:

Table 8
Cost Estimates for Option 2

Parameters	Cost Estimates
NJ Transit Operating cost per vehicle-hour[1]	$129
Required number of buses to match hourly train arrival/departure schedule	2
Operating span per day (hours)	12
Number of operating days (Weekends, Holidays – Memorial Day through Labor day)	34
Operating cost per day	$3,096
Operating cost per season	$105,264
Marketing Costs	~ $20,000
Reservation System Costs	~ $50,000

Option 4: Local Resident Bicycle Incentive Program and Connection of the Henry Hudson Trail to the Sandy Hook Multi-Use Pathway

The relevant parameters and cost estimates (rough) are presented below:

Table 9
Cost Estimates for Option 4

Parameters	Cost Estimates
Estimate of daily usage (bicyclists participating in program per weekend day)	100-300
Number of operating days (Weekends, Holidays – Memorial day through Labor Day)	34
Reverse fee or rebate per participant	$5
Incentive Program 'cost' per day	$500-$1,500
Incentive Program 'cost' per operating season	$17,000-$51,000
Administration (bar-code registration)	~ $5,000
Pc-based software MIS	~ $25,000
Planning, design and construction of missing link on Henry Hudson Trail	TBD (could run between ~ $100,000- $3M, depending on proportion of off-road to on-road segments, and whether need acquisition of ROW

Alternative Access Options Rejected

Other planning processes[*] have suggested either a series of bus shuttle services from each of the Bayshore/Route 36 corridor towns to Sandy Hook during summer tourist season, or from Middletown Train Station, Keansburg Amusement park, and the ferry terminals at Atlantic Highlands and Highlands. From the towns, the bus shuttles would use existing school or other public parking lots as park-and-ride or staging areas. The town-based shuttle system concept has NOT been advocated in this plan for several reasons:

- Local usage alone from the towns would be insufficient to have a high frequency quality service

- Routing of the buses is along the same congested Route 36 corridor and would yield no travel time savings to the visitor

- The distributed set of small park-and-ride staging areas makes diversion of visitors from outside the region complex and inefficient

- A sizeable number of buses would need to be deployed to provide even a minimal level-of-service and frequency

The *Sandy Hook- Route 36 Corridor Summer Traffic Management and Agency Coordination Plan* proffered a very serious and interesting system of local and express routes (see Figure 18 below).

---

[*] See, e.g., Monmouth County Planning Board, *Bayshore Region Strategic Plan*, 2006; also, see *Sandy Hook – Route 36 Corridor Summer Traffic Management Plan*, February 2001.

Figure 18
Proposed Bayshore Shuttle Bus Service
Source: Sandy Hook-Route 36 Corridor Summer Traffic Management and Agency Coordination Plan

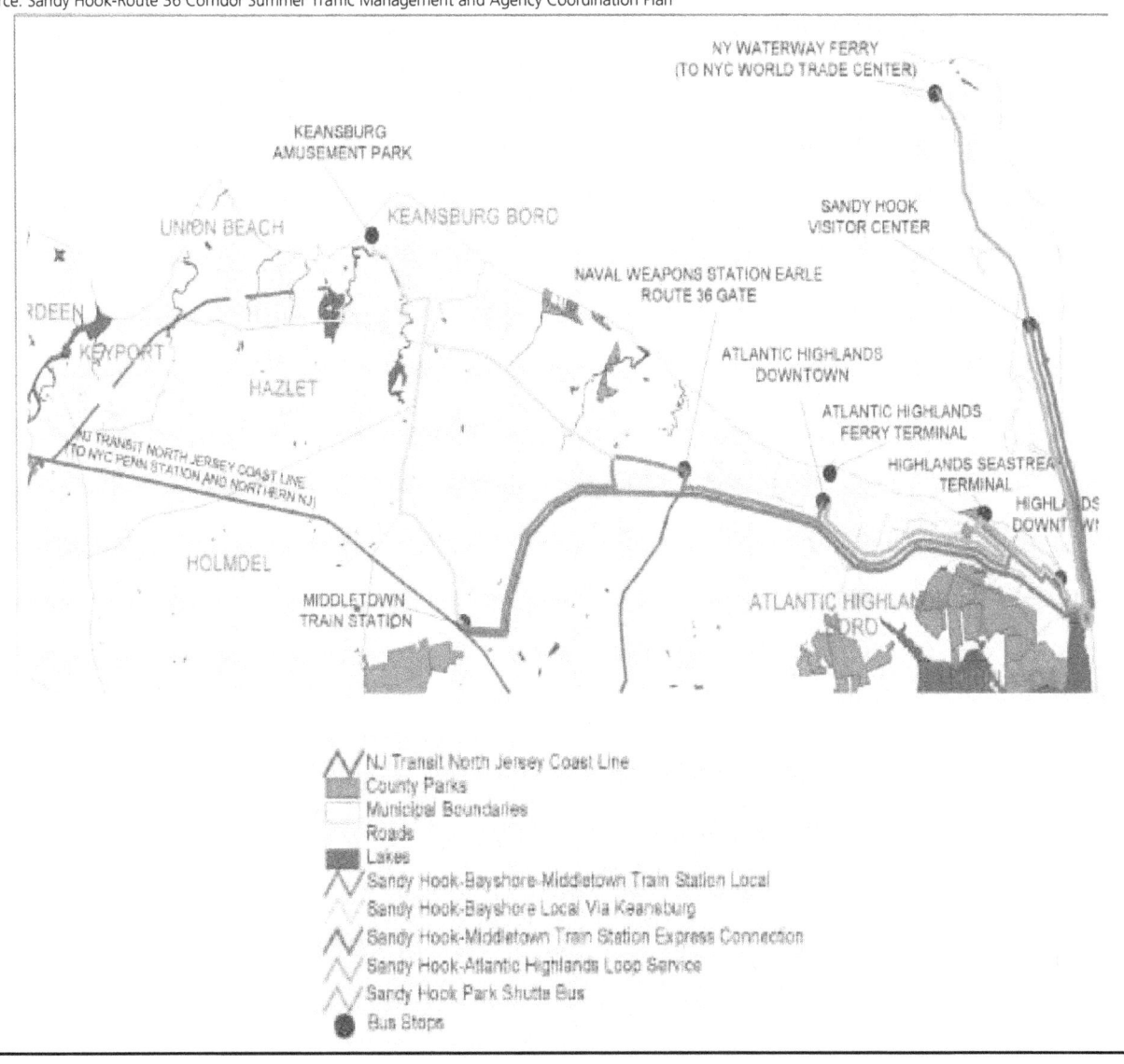

However, this proposal too suffers some of the same defects:

- Routing of buses along the same congested Route 36 corridor, with unreliable service and no savings in travel time for the visitor

- Connection to the intra-park shuttle requiring an additional transfer and wait

- Service of markets with insufficient demand to support a high-quality, high-frequency service

- No site proposed for the interceptor lots off of Route 36 (i.e., proposal incomplete)

The exception is the proposed Express Bus service linking Middletown Train station (thereby serving the NYC market) to Sandy Hook. This report proposes Option 2: NJ Transit Coordinated Train/Bus Shuttle Service to Sandy Hook as a modification and improvement to this previous concept in several respects:

- Connection at the Red Bank Train Station, permitting a better routing of the bus shuttle that avoids the severe congestion along the Route 36 corridor, although there is no escape from delays and congestion along the routing proposed through Rumson (County Route 520, the Rumson Bridge and Ocean Avenue)

- Coordinated scheduling of the train and bus shuttle on arrival and departure from the region

- Reserved seating for the combined travel package

- Bus shuttle penetration of Sandy Hook and provision of distributor/collector service at all beaches

- Avoidance of transfer and wait for the intra-park shuttle

Extension of the NJ Transit bus lines 834 and 835 to connect to Sandy Hook has also been rejected as a viable concept. Reasons include:

- For same reasons as above, the Route 36 corridor routing is problematic

- Frequency of service is quite low (~ 1 hour headways) to be an attractive service and would require additional buses to even maintain this low frequency of service

- Inability to capture NYC market, or diversion of regional visitors off of GSP or along Route 36

- Requirement of additional transfer to, and wait for, the intra-park shuttle

The Intra-Park Shuttle – Ideas for Vehicle Replacement

The ferry operator (SeaStreak) lands at Ft. Hancock, on the opposite side of the peninsula from the major beaches. As a condition of its right to land at Sandy Hook, the ferry operator is obligated to provide an intra-park shuttle that provides a distributor/collector transit service to/from the ferry dock landing and the beaches at Sandy Hook.

At this point (2009), both the dock and the intra-park shuttle are operated and controlled by the ferry operator. The operating cost is small relative to the daily operating cost for the ferry (~ 3 percent according to cost estimates provided by SeaStreak), but it does add to the required per person round-trip fare and is also an institutional obstacle to the addition of other ferry services provided by other operators. It is NOT clear whether the existing ferry operator is required to allow other potential ferry operators access to the intra-park shuttle (even with compensation) or would use the system as a competitive 'weapon' to bar other operators. If these other operators have to replicate a similar intra-park transit service, it would be inefficient and costly and could lead to unnecessary congestion at the loading/unloading points.

The park is planning (hopefully by the 2010 season) to own and maintain a new ferry dock (and dismantle the old ferry dock). This could as a matter of policy reduce the barge landing fees to all operators thereby encouraging other operators (by reducing the price of entry as well as not allowing a competitive edge to any one operator) to provide ferry service from other embarkation points along the New Jersey Bayshore and Route 36 corridor and from NYC. Once the park owns and maintains the dock, the park can open up the dock for access to other operators by negotiating agreements for the public good. At this point, it is in our opinion untenable that the intra-park shuttle continue to be controlled by a private ferry operator who also is a competitor to the other ferry operators serving Sandy Hook. Once the park controls the dock, it has little choice but to also control (NOT necessarily operate) the other piece of infrastructure, i.e., the intra-park shuttle. The new dock is essentially at the same location as the old dock, because other potential site locations that might be closer to the main beaches via walking mode and reduce the need for an intra-park shuttle are not viable because of the sensitive ecology of the shore. It is also desirable in the long-term for the park to control the intra-park shuttle in order for the system to best serve the needs of the re-utilized Ft. Hancock development[*]

The current intra-park shuttle system comprises two routes: a northern route serving Ft. Hancock, Gunnison and North beach, and a southern route serving the other beaches and Sea Gull's nest dining area, and the Visitor's Center. This is an efficient network design. It partitions the system into two equal transit time circuits to/from the ferry dock of approximately 15-20 minutes. The alternative of a single, combined route serving all beaches would result in excessively long travel times for the visitor. One vehicle – currently a school bus – is deployed to each of the two routes.

At the ferry dock, each ferry arrival discharges a large group of visitors. Because of the popularity of Gunnison Beach (a "clothing-optional" beach), demand for access via the northern route exceeds a single bus load. Visitors either have to wait for a second bus run on the northern route or else walk. About half of the visitors discharged at the dock walk in any case. The southern route rarely exceeds a single bus load after the ferry discharges its passengers. Multiple runs on the northern route are also often required to bring visitors back to the dock for the ferry departures.

---

[*] See *Environmental Assessment: Adaptive Use of Fort Hancock and the Sandy Hook Proving Ground Historic District*, February 2002, revised July 2003.

The existing school buses are certainly adequate from a pure transportation operations perspective. They have and are currently working to disperse passengers from the ferry dock landing to/from the beaches. There are some issues, however, with the existing buses that could be mitigated by replacement:

- Lack of compatibility with a high-quality visitor experience in a beach environment

- Lack of ADA compatibility

- Time-consuming and difficult passenger loading/unloading at stops (tight rows of seats, and inadequate number of doors)

- Interior and exterior noise, and air emissions are high and disturbing to visitors and roadside fauna

- Inadequate bus unit capacity for northern route deployment

Project staff determined from an on-site visit that a class of replacement vehicles which ordinarily would be a good choice for a beach environment – open-air rubber-tired trams – is NOT a feasible replacement vehicle at Sandy Hook. Both the volume and particularly the speeds (45 mph speed limit, with actual operating speeds often approaching 55 mph) on Hartshorne Drive, the main access to/from the beach parking lots, pose an undue safety hazard for a slow, articulated tram with one or more passenger-carrying trailer units.

A potential class of replacement vehicles compatible with the operating environment at Sandy Hook and capable of resolving the issues associated with the current fleet of school buses is hybrid (diesel-electric) urban transit buses. For the northern route, our recommendation would be to deploy an articulated 60-foot hybrid (diesel-electric) bus. NPS staff provided the existing routing of the school buses on the roads at Sandy Hook. Project staff tested the ability of a specific model in this class (the New Flyer DE60LF – see Figure 19) to negotiate the tight turns at several critical intersections on the route. The results are illustrated in Figure 19. A 60-foot articulated bus can provide the requisite bus capacity needed to satisfy the demand for access on the northern route and still negotiate the route. For the southern route, a 40-foot hybrid (diesel-electric) urban transit bus is sufficient in bus capacity.

Figure 19
A New Flyer DE60LF in Albuquerque, NM
Source: http://en.wikipedia.org (Author PerryPlanet released photo to public domain)

Figure 20
Results of New Flyer DE60LF in negotiating the tight turns at several critical intersections on the route
Source: Imagery provided by NJ DOT, data provided by Sandy Hook (modified by the Volpe Center)

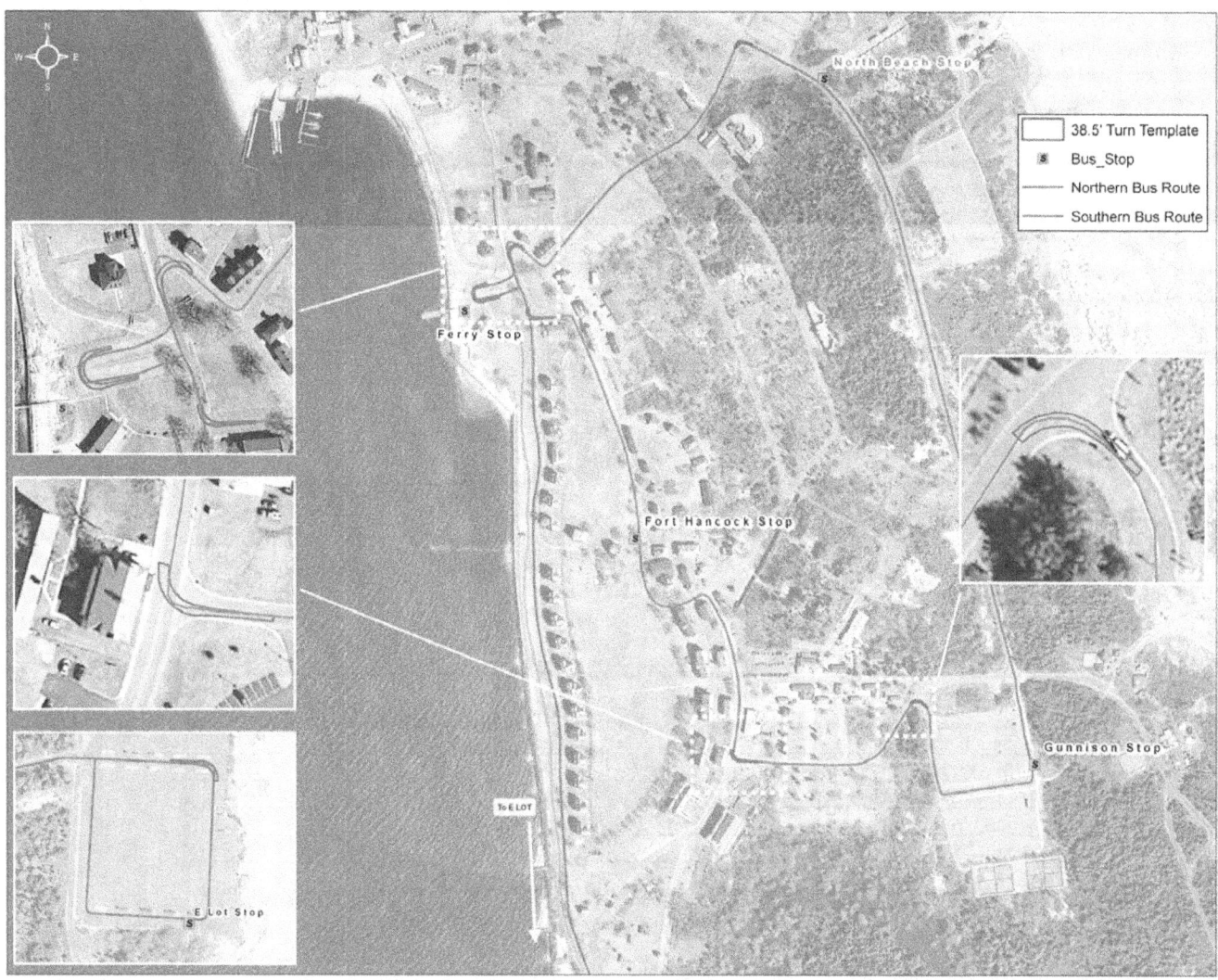

Another reason why the New Flyer DE60LF is a particularly good choice within this class for Sandy Hook is that there is substantial good operating experience with this bus by transit authorities. Tables 10 & 11 below illustrate a systematic evaluation at King County Metro in Seattle of a fleet of diesel articulated versus hybrid articulated New Flyer buses, both fleets acquired at the same time from New Flyer and operated under similar duty cycles. Most importantly, the non-hybrid version (the D60LF) is currently operated by Academy Bus Lines under contract to Rutgers University on the Rutgers University Campus bus shuttle system. Discussion with Academy Bus Lines indicates that they have both the technical, organizational and operating experience to migrate to and operate and maintain the hybrid version. Project staff sees a great opportunity for a three-way partnership (see the section on Next Steps below) between Sandy Hook, Rutgers University and their contractor – Academy Bus Lines. Under the Transit in the Park (TRIP) program, Sandy Hook could acquire and own the 60-foot articulated and 40-foot hybrid buses. These buses would then be leased for $1 per annum to Rutgers University to be operated during the academic year on the Rutgers University bus shuttle system. Rutgers University in turn would assume the operating and maintenance costs of the buses when deployed on the intra-park shuttle system between

Memorial Day and Labor Day. Academy Bus Lines – the Rutgers University Contractor – would be the organization that actually operates the service and maintains and stores the vehicles.

Tables 10 & 11
Summary Evaluation Results and Hybrid vs. Convention Bus Test Results

Source: K. Chandler and K. Walkowicz, *King County Metro Transit Hybrid Articulated Buses Final Evaluation Results*, Technical Report NREL/TP-540-40585, December 2006.

Table ES-2. Summary Evaluation Results (12-month evaluation period)

Category	Diesel Ryerson Base	Hybrid Atlantic Base	Hybrid Difference	Hybrid South Base
Monthly Average Mileage per Bus	2,949	3,096	+5%	3,957
Fuel Economy (mpg)	2.50	3.17	+27%	3.75
Fuel Cost per Mile ($) (@$1.98/gal)	0.79	0.62	-22%	0.53
Total Maintenance Cost per Mile ($)	0.46	0.44	-4%	0.41
Propulsion-Only Maintenance Cost per Mile ($)	0.12	0.13	+8%	0.13
Total Operating Cost per Mile ($)	1.25	1.06	-15%	0.94
Miles Between All Road calls	5,896	4,954	-16%	4,696
Miles Between Propulsion Road calls	12,199	10,616	-13%	8,547

Ryerson, Atlantic, and South are all depots for King County Metro. Results for hybrid buses operating out of the South Base appear in gray type because those vehicles have a higher operating average speed than the other two depots and should not be used in direct comparison.

Table ES-3. Hybrid Bus vs. Conventional Bus Test Results

	Manhattan	OCTA	CBD	KCM	In-use: Atlantic Base
Fuel Economy (mpg, % increase)	74.6%	50.6%	48.3%	30.3%	26.8%
Fuel Consumption (gram/mi, % reduction)	42.9%	33.7%	32.8%	23.4%	21.2%
NOx (gpm, % reduction)	38.7%	28.6%	26.6%	17.8%	-
PM (gpm, % reduction)	92.6%	50.8%	97.1%	Ns	-
CO (gpm, % reduction)	ns	32.0%	48.0%	59.5%	-
THC (gpm, % reduction)	ns	ns	75.2%	56.3%	-

Note: gpm = gallons per mile; mpg = miles per gallon; ns = not statistically significant at 95% confidence level or not enough data to determine; THC = total hydrocarbon.

The second table indicates differences in measurements between the hybrid and conventional diesel bus (so percent increase or reduction from diesel to hybrid). The columns refer to different driving cycles for the buses: Manhattan, the Orange County Transit Authority (OCTA), Central Business District 14 (CBD), a custom cycle made up of various King County runs (KCM), and the current hybrid run out of the Atlantic depot.

Next Steps

There are a number of recommended 'next steps' for Sandy Hook engagement. These are summarized below:

- Meet with Teri O'Connor, Monmouth County, to discuss issuance of a request for proposal (RFP) for new ferry service from Belford Ferry Terminal to Sandy Hook during weekends and holidays (Memorial Day through Labor Day); assuming a positive response of bidders from potential ferry operators, work with Monmouth County to set public hearing and agenda item for vote by the Aldermen

- Meet with New Jersey Transportation Planning Authority (NJTPA) – the MPO – to seek CMAQ funds for a 3-year pilot 'demo' of the new ferry service from Belford Ferry Terminal to Sandy Hook to underwrite the cost in order to lower the per passenger round-trip fare to a level more competitive with access by private vehicle. The case should be made on the basis of congestion relief – the removal of cars from the congested, over-saturated Route 36 corridor – rather than air quality improvement to the regional air shed. Unfortunately, ferries tend to be quite fuel-consumptive and 'dirty', having a high carbon footprint.[*]

- Meet with both the Monmouth County Parks and Recreation Department and the New Jersey Transportation Planning Authority (NJTPA) – the MPO – to seek Transportation Enhancement (TE) Funds to complete the missing segment of the Henry Hudson Trail that connects the existing terminus at Avenue D in Atlantic Highlands to the approach to the Reconstructed Highlands Bridge. Work on the missing segment would include all phases including planning, design, public process and construction. This would provide the missing link for local bike and pedestrian access to Sandy Hook since the new bridge will include bicycle lanes that connect via a flyover to the Multi-User Path (MUP) at Sandy Hook.

- Seek Paul S. Sarbanes Transit in Parks Program (TRIP – formerly ATPPL) funds to develop the bar-code and PC-based management information system to implement the local resident Incentive Program for bicycle access to Sandy Hook.

- Seek TRIP funds to pursue a public planning process in collaboration with Monmouth County Parks and Recreation Department and to develop 25-percent alternative designs and visualizations of Option 5: Redesign of the Henry Hudson Multi-Use Trail for Tram Operation.

- Meet with State Agencies whose principal responsibility is economic development and tourism, and with NJ Transit to encourage these agencies to develop a new travel package – Option 2- consisting of a coordinated and combined train and connector bus service to Sandy Hook via the NJ Train Coast Line to Red Bank Station. NJ Transit would develop the marketing plan and materials, including reservation system, and conduct outreach for the service and would deploy buses and schedule and operate the bus shuttle. Fares for the combined package would reflect the normal system-wide fare-box recovery ratio for the bus shuttle component, with the State of New Jersey subsidizing the remaining costs of the bus shuttle component.

- Conduct a one-day workshop at the park with NJ Transit bus operations and maintenance specialists (as independent peer reviewers), Academy Bus Lines, and Rutgers University staff with oversight and management responsibility for the Rutgers University Campus Bus Shuttle System. The purpose of the workshop is threefold: (1) ground test the New Flyer D60LF articulated bus

---

[*] J. Corbett, A. Farrell, D. Redman and J. Winebrake, *Air Pollution from Passenger Ferries in New York Harbor*, July 2003.

used at Rutgers University to confirm that the articulated bus can easily negotiate the northern intra-park shuttle route; (2) confirm that both the articulated 60-foot hybrid bus (diesel-electric) and the 40-foot hybrid bus (diesel-electric) articulated in this concept-plan as potentially good choices for vehicle replacement are in fact suitable for the application, including duty cycle and environmental conditions (i.e., sea-shore high moisture and salt environment) found at Sandy Hook; and (3) assuming a positive confirmation, develop a negotiated partnership framework among Rutgers University, Academy Bus Lines and the park.

- Seek TRIP funds to acquire the two new buses – the articulated 60-foot hybrid (diesel-electric) bus and the 40-foot hybrid (diesel-electric) bus - for the intra-park shuttle system. The buses would be shared between the park and Rutgers University, with the University and Academy Bus Lines assuming their respective roles in sustaining the operation (including storage and maintenance of the buses) in accordance with the negotiated partnership framework. This partnership framework is the critical piece in increasing the competiveness of the park's project to acquire new buses.

References

B. Hemily and R. King, *Use of Higher-Capacity Buses in Transit Service*, TCRP Synthesis 75, 2008.
http://onlinepubs.trb.org/onlinepubs/tcrp/tcrp_syn_75.pdf

K. Chandler and K. Walkowicz, *King County Metro Transit Hybrid Articulated Buses Final Evaluation Results*, National Renewable Energy Laboratory. Technical Report NREL/TP-540-40585. December 2006.
http://www.nrel.gov/vehiclesandfuels/fleettest/pdfs/40585.pdf

Environmental Assessment: Adaptive Use of Fort Hancock and the Sandy Hook Proving Ground Historic District, February 2002, revised July 2003.

Monmouth County Planning Board, *Bayshore Region Strategic Plan*, September 2006.
http://co.monmouth.nj.us/documents%5C24%5CBayshore%20Region%20Strategic%20Plan.pdf

Monmouth County Planning Board. *Sandy Hook – Route 36 Corridor Summer Traffic Management and Agency Coordination Plan*, February 2001.
http://co.monmouth.nj.us/documents%5C24%5CSandy%20Hook%20RT36%20Corridor%20Study.pdf

JE/Sverdrup and Parcel Consultants, Inc., *Gateway Village Rehabilitation Project: Traffic Impact Study*, 2003.

Rails-to-Trails Conservancy, *Rails with Trails: Design, Management, and Operating Characteristics of 61 Trails along Active Rail Lines*, November 2000.
http://www.railstotrails.org/resources/documents/resource_docs/Rails-with-Trails%20Report%20reprint_1-06_lr.pdf

US Department of Transportation, *Rails-with-Trails: Lessons Learned. Literature review, Current Practices, Conclusions*, August 2002.
http://www.fhwa.dot.gov/environment/RecTrails/rwt/railswithtrails.pdf

J. Corbett, A. Farrell, D. Redman and J. Winebrake, *Air Pollution from Passenger Ferries in New York Harbor*, July 2003. http://www.bluewaternetwork.org/reports/rep_ss_nyreport.pdf

REPORT DOCUMENTATION PAGE

Form Approved
OMB No. 0704 0188

The public reporting burden for this collection of information is estimated to average 1 hour per response, including the time for reviewing instructions, searching existing data sources, gathering and maintaining the data needed, and completing and reviewing the collection of information. Send comments regarding this burden estimate or any other aspect of this collection of information, including suggestions for reducing the burden, to Department of Defense, Washington Headquarters Services, Directorate for Information Operations and Reports (0704-0188), 1215 Jefferson Davis Highway, Suite 1204, Arlington, VA 22202-4302. Respondents should be aware that notwithstanding any other provision of law, no person shall be subject to any penalty for failing to comply with a collection of information if it does not display a currently valid OMB control number.
PLEASE DO NOT RETURN YOUR FORM TO THE ABOVE ADDRESS.

1. REPORT DATE (DD MM YYYY)	2. REPORT TYPE	3. DATES COVERED (From To)
xx-06-09	Transportation Planning Study	October 2008-June 2009

4. TITLE AND SUBTITLE

Sandy Hook: Alternative Access Concept Plan and Vehicle Replacement Study

5a. CONTRACT NUMBER

F4505087777

5b. GRANT NUMBER

5c. PROGRAM ELEMENT NUMBER

6. AUTHOR(S)

Spiller, David J., and Fisher, Frances.

5d. PROJECT NUMBER

PMIS No. 133841A

5e. TASK NUMBER

5f. WORK UNIT NUMBER

7. PERFORMING ORGANIZATION NAME(S) AND ADDRESS(ES)

U.S. Department of Transportation
Research and Innovative Transportation Administration
John A. Volpe National Transportation Systems Center
55 Broadway, Cambridge, MA 02142

8. PERFORMING ORGANIZATION REPORT NUMBER

DOT-VNTSC-NPS-09-01

9. SPONSORING/MONITORING AGENCY NAME(S) AND ADDRESS(ES)

U.S. Department of the Interior
National Park Service
Northeast Region
15 State Street, Boston, MA 02109

10. SPONSOR/MONITOR'S ACRONYM(S)

NPS NER & GATE

11. SPONSOR/MONITOR'S REPORT NUMBER(S)

D-100028

12. DISTRIBUTION/AVAILABILITY STATEMENT

Public distribution/availability

13. SUPPLEMENTARY NOTES

This report addresses alternative transportation decision factors as indicated below (Y/N/NA):
(Y) Non-construction options; (N) park carrying capacity; (N) life-cycle/ops. & maintenance costs; (N) cost-effectiveness.

14. ABSTRACT

This study addresses two critical issues of concern to the Sandy Hook Unit of Gateway National Recreational Area: (1) options for alternative access to Sandy Hook during peak summer season, particularly when the park is closed to private vehicles when parking facilities are full; and (2) options for a replacement vehicle for the intra-park shuttle that carries passengers disembarking from the ferry to the beaches.

15. SUBJECT TERMS

national park, park, alternative transportation, transportation, ferry, shuttle

16. SECURITY CLASSIFICATION OF:			17. LIMITATION OF ABSTRACT	18. NUMBER OF PAGES	19a. NAME OF RESPONSIBLE PERSON
a. REPORT	b. ABSTRACT	c. THIS PAGE	NA	47	Peter Steele, NER & Hollis Provins, GATE
None	None	None			19b. TELEPHONE NUMBER (Include area code) 617-223-5130, NER & 732-872-5932, GATE

Standard Form 298 (Rev. 8/98)
Prescribed by ANSI Std. Z39.18

www.ingramcontent.com/pod-product-compliance
Lightning Source LLC
Chambersburg PA
CBHW080448290526
45791CB00008BA/2646

* 9 7 8 1 4 9 4 8 7 1 3 8 3 *